EXITING THI

YOGA

on the YELLOW
the BRICK ROAD

CALM YOUR MIND

ALAN STEELMAN

POWERED BY

black card
B O O K S

Author: Alan Steelman
Title: Yoga on the Yellow Brick Road
ISBN: 978-1-77204-995-4
Category: SELF-HELP/Self-Management/Stress Management

Publisher: Black Card Books
Division of Gerry Robert Enterprises Inc.
Suite 214, 5-18 Ringwood Drive
Stouffville, Ontario, Canada, L4A 0N2
International Calling: +1 877 280 8536
www.blackcardbooks.com

....

EXITING THE A.S.A.P. LANE!

YOGA
on the YELLOW
BRICK ROAD

CALM YOUR MIND

ALAN STEELMAN

POWERED BY

black card
B O O K S

Heal the World

Dalai Lama

"If meditation was taught to every eight-year-old,
we could eliminate all violence from the world in one generation."

— ❦ —

Dr. Melanie Greenberg

"Mindfulness has the potential to make not only individuals,
but businesses, institutions, and societies stress-proof."

— ❦ —

**The Honorable Tim Ryan,
U.S. House of Representatives (D-Ohio)**

"Stress is optional... we can become a mindful nation."

Endorsements

"How often do we hear coaches and athletes talk about the need to 'slow the game down'? Is it only a coincidence that recent Super Bowl and NBA championship winning teams also incorporate yoga into their team training regimens? With the game on the line, this becomes essential. For elite athletes, successful coaches and all of us, self-control is fundamental to making the smartest decisions. In this book, Alan Steelman provides a disciplined approach for all us that would vastly improve our ability to cope with the pace of life today."

—Joe Bailey
Former COO, National Football League World League, www.nfl.com
CEO, Miami Dolphins, www.miamidolphins.com

"During perilous times like these, screaming panic may seem like the only rational option. Meditation and yoga, according to Alan Steelman, offer something better. He says they're the key to a calm mind, which means I can recommend his book to all the Americans whose minds are understandably agitated. If their minds were calmer, mine would be, too, and maybe a gentle peace would descend on our troubled land. I'm pretty sure it wouldn't make things worse."

—Steve Chapman
Columnist and Editorial Writer
Member of Editorial Board, *Chicago Tribune*
www.chicagotribune.com

"The quest for 'bigger, better, faster, stronger' is a good descriptor for the lives many of us lead today, and this can have a negative impact on our physical and mental health, relationships, and the way we live in the world. In this book about *Life in the A.S.A.P. Lane!*, Alan Steelman outlines the tragic national consequences of such a stressful way of living. Record-high opioid overdose deaths, soaring obesity rates, and alarmingly high teen anxiety and suicide attempts all illuminate the depth and breadth of this problem. The good news, Alan says, is that 'there is an exit ramp'. He calls it the Yellow Brick Road, referring to mindful breathing. In my book, *The Stress-Proof Brain*, I say that mindfulness has the potential to make not only individuals, but businesses, institutions, and societies stress-proof. Read Alan's book, it is your path to a healthier mind and body."

—Dr. Melanie Greenberg
Author of Bestselling Book, *The Stress-Proof Brain*
Practicing Psychologist, Speaker, and Life/Business Coach

"Alan Steelman has had remarkable success in business and politics. His mantra is '*Mens sana in corpora sana*' (a healthy mind in a healthy body), and in this book, he reveals the path to the inner balance required for a healthy, successful life. For years, I've listened to Alan Steelman—a 'renaissance man', if ever there was one. In this book, he reveals the true path to success, longevity, and balance. This is a worthy guide book."

—Bob Lutz
Former Vice-Chairman, General Motors, www.gm.com
Iconic International Auto Executive and Bestselling Author of *Car Guys vs Bean Counters*, *Icons and Idiots* and *Guts: 8 Laws of Business from One of the Most Innovative Business Leaders of Our Time*
www.boblutzsez.com

"We are inundated with information every day. Between smartphones, the Internet, television we are moving ever faster every day, yet we always feel like we are falling further behind. Back in 2012, I wrote *A Mindful Nation* to help everyday Americans capture the power of mindful meditation, a proven practice that can help us slow down and reconnect. Today, we need these practices more than ever. As Alan Steelman, a former member of Congress says, 'There is an exit ramp—a practice of yoga and meditation.' These practices are an integral part of my daily routine, and the best part is anyone can benefit from them."

—Congressman Tim Ryan (D-Ohio)
Author of *The Mindful Nation* and *The Real Food Revolution*
Leading authority in the United States Congress on mindfulness
and its national healing potential
www.timryan.house.gov

———— ✄ ————

"This book is refreshing to read. I'm proof there IS an exit ramp, as the book calls it, off the A.S.A.P. Lane. The pace of life today makes most all of us anxious, stressed, and pressured, no matter our job or family situation. Tragically, an increasing number are finding that they can't cope without using substances that are destructive to their health. Read this book and you will find a regimen that will help you immensely. In addition to my professional career, I have taught yoga and continue to practice on a regular basis. It can truly change your life."

—Dawn Scott
Emmy Award and Edward R. Murrow Award winning
CBS-affiliate News Anchor
Producer and anchor of the Emmy Award-winning, *A Place Called Home*,
featuring children up for adoption
www.lifeofatvmom.blogspot.com

"My life was dramatically changed, if not saved, by discovering yoga. In addition to the normal yoga instruction classes that I lead at yoga studios, I devote a considerable amount of my time, introducing yoga to school age boys and girls, and adults who may not fit the traditional stereotype of a yoga practitioner. Anxiety, stress, and pressure are ever-present companions in our lives in today's world. The artificial crutches that so many are using to cope can be avoided. I highly recommend that you read this book, and start on your own journey of self-regulating your own health."

—**Ebony Smith**
Founder of Yoga N Da Hood, www.yogandahood.com
Emerging national leader in taking mindfulness
to underserved communities and people

———— ✂ ————

"Former U.S. Congressman Alan Steelman states that the mental health crisis has reached epidemic proportions, as evidenced by record levels of opioid overdoses, binge alcohol consumption, and obesity levels. Peace of mind and better health may seem like a huge task at this moment, but it is worth it and you will thank yourself forever when you realize that you can still participate in life FULL OUT, and do so without relying on artificial stimulants. You decided to open this book. You decided to read this far. You now get to decide to put these ideas into action and your decision will manifest in better physical and mental health—almost immediately."

—**Barry Spilchuk**
Co-author of International Bestseller *A Cup of Chicken Soup for the Soul*
Founder of www.TheLEGACY.club

"This is not just a book about yoga—this is a work of heart. Alan's passion for encouraging others to give yoga a try comes not from any agenda, but from his own unexpected experience of discovering the real beauty of this ancient healing system. Not only has he done his research, he has done his outreach—speaking to a variety of "unconventional" students to ensure his perspective is authentic and valid. It certainly is."

—Charla and David Truesdale
Co-founders of the Warrior Spirit Project™ (WSP)
www.warriorspiritproject.org
WSP was founded on the premise that a
"broken spirit can be more harmful than a broken body".
David is a 27-year veteran of service in the Naval Criminal Investigative Service,
including stints in both Afghanistan and Iraq.
Charla has 25 years of experience in wellness and military culture.
Both served a deployment at GITMO.

"No matter where you are on your journey of life, yoga can help you achieve your goals with more ease, grace and stamina. Many people know about the powerful physical practices, but more and more people are tuning in to a deeper power of the yoga practice: the breath. Alan's beautiful metaphors of the breath, based on the beloved story of *The Wizard of Oz*, draws you in to a deeper understanding of how to find ease in your life through yoga. Alan lays out a regimen for the beginner, regardless of age or physical fitness level that will get you on your very own path to better health and more peace."

—Lauren Walker
Author of *Energy Medicine Yoga: Amplify the Healing Power of Your Yoga Practice*
and *The Energy Medicine Yoga Prescription*
A Highly-innovative Thinker and Teacher
One of the Top 100 Most Influential Yoga Teachers in America

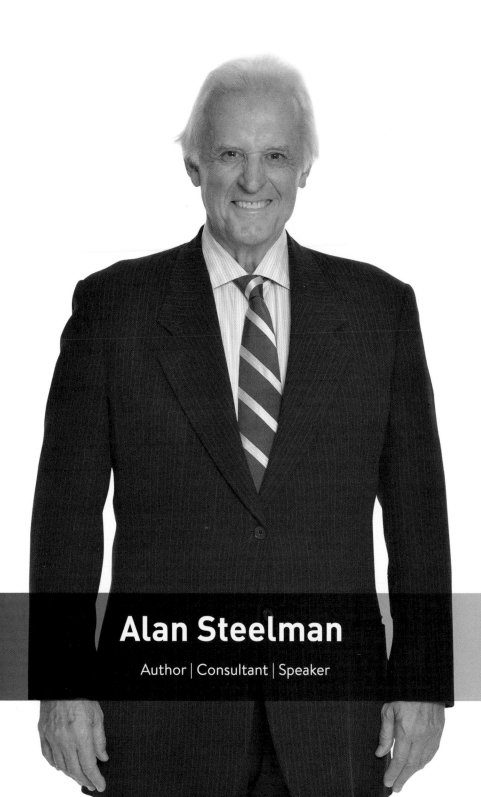

Alan Steelman

Author | Consultant | Speaker

About the Author

Alan Steelman is a former Member of the U.S. Congress (R-Texas), Former Vice Chairman of Alexander Proudfoot Company, and former Chairman of the Dallas Council on World Affairs. He has served on the Board of Directors of Sterling Software (NYSE), Aristocrat Technologies (ASX), and the Texas Growth Fund. He is a graduate of Baylor University, holds an MLA degree from Southern Methodist University, and was a Resident Fellow at the Institute of Politics at Harvard University. He is a certified yoga instructor.

His career in politics was marked with distinction. He was the youngest Member of Congress when he was elected. *Time* magazine named him one of the top 200 Young Emerging Leaders in America in a special issue devoted to leadership in America. In endorsing his re-election, the *Dallas Times Herald* called him one of the best ever sent to Congress from Texas. *Texas Monthly* named him among the top five of the most effective members of the 24-person Texas Congressional Delegation, and *New Times* named him one of the top "10 Best Congressmen" in the country during his second term.

His global business career, which spanned 35 years, included an 8-year stint in Singapore as President of the Asia-Pacific region for Alexander Proudfoot, and culminated in his serving as Vice Chairman of the company and Chairman of the Board of Advisors, a global group of former Fortune 500 company Chief Executives.

Born in Little Rock, Arkansas, he is married to his wife, Susan, formerly Susan Seligman Fuller, and is the father of five children: Robin Whitehead, Kim Cuban, Allison Steelman, Alan Steelman, Jr., and Alex Steelman. He is the stepfather of two: Daniel Fuller and Elizabeth Fuller.

Dedication

I am grateful for the support of my wife, Susan, through the long laborious process of writing this book.

My adoption and continuing practice of yoga has been influenced by a number of people. My initial inspiration came from my son, Alex, who was already a disciplined fitness devotee, but told me that he had found something different in yoga that wasn't easy to explain, but was profound.

My first instructor, Michael Festauti, who remains my primary instructor for all my Power Yoga sessions. In addition, Michael and his daughter, Nicole Allen, who run Space Yoga in Dallas, led me through the intense and rigorous 200-hour course necessary to become an officially certified yoga instructor.

I want to thank my three fellow students, Nola O' Donnell, Dr. Cynthia Manzano, and Alex Worsham with whom I shared the certification course instruction, and who gave me the first positive response to linking yoga to the Yellow Brick Road and the Wizard of Oz story.

To my children, Robin, Kim, Allison, Alan, Jr. and the aforementioned, Alex, you have been my greatest gift, and you have my unconditional love. To my stepdaughter, Elizabeth Fuller for her input, and serving as a valuable sounding board along the way.

Virtually every word of this was written at either the Starbucks store in Highland Park Village or the Royal Blue Grocery store at the same location, in my hometown of Dallas. I owe a special debt of gratitude to Jan Weiser, the manager of the Starbucks store, and her amazing team and to Zac and Emily Porter, owners of the Royal Blue. Neither ever charged me rent and have been very accommodating every step of the way.

Finally, anything written on the topic of yoga stands on the shoulders of over 5,000 years of tradition, writings, and a continuing evolution of a practice and discipline that brings added strength, balance and flexibility—but, most of all, a calm mind.

Foreword

by Barry Spilchuk

Co-author of International Bestseller *A Cup of Chicken Soup for the Soul*

Founder of www.TheLEGACY.club

If you are going to climb a local hill to help you cope with a personal health or lifestyle challenge, it's probably okay to try it alone as long as you are physically able. However, if your challenge is threatening your health and well-being and has become a personal Mount Everest, that's a different story.

Congratulations on taking the next step to conquering what has become a mountain for more and more of us coping with increasing levels of anxiety, stress, pressure, and, for many among us, addiction to health-destroying substances. As we get older (and hopefully wiser), we realize the old adage "without your health, you don't have much". If you're like me, challenged by an appetite for food, you may have tried the diets, the infomercial quick fixes (that are gathering dust with the cellophane still on the box), the pills, the powders, and the magic elixirs. Somehow, those solutions didn't work the way we had hoped they would.

One of the secrets that I confess to is, those programs won't work unless I do! (I knew there was a catch!)

This new journey that you are on WILL WORK this time. How do I know? One reason is, you purchased this book! That's the first sign that you're on the right road—the Yellow Brick Road. Another reason I know it will be effective this time is because your personal guide, your Sherpa, is Alan Steelman.

Former U.S. Congressman Alan Steelman is dedicated to starting a movement throughout his home state of Texas, across America, and around the world. As he states in the first chapter, the mental health crisis in the United States has reached epidemic proportions, as evidenced by record levels of opioid overdoses, binge alcohol consumption, and obesity levels. I have always loved the premise that ONE thought can change your world and ONE action can start an avalanche of change.

Peace of mind and better health may seem like a huge task at this moment, but it is worth it, and you will thank yourself forever when you realize that you can still participate in life FULL OUT, and do so without relying on artificial stimulants.

It starts with a decision. You decided to open this book. You decided to read this far. You now get to decide to put these ideas into action, and your decision will manifest in better physical and mental health—almost immediately.

The cost to you: A little gentle effort!

Alan has lovingly embraced the challenge of making this book entertaining, educational, spiritual, and factual. Some of you will jump right in and enjoy the immediate and long-term benefits of yoga and meditation. Some will enjoy the stories, while a few more of you will want to know the facts and research that support the claims that yoga and meditation can help you heal.

It's all here.

As I got to know Alan, I was honored to share every moment with him. I've been blessed to speak in front of thousands of authors. I have had the privilege of coaching dozens and dozens of authors one-on-one. Never in my 23-year history of working with books have I ever met someone who is so open to coaching, feedback, and guidance.

One of the reasons he was such an effective and admired congressman is his ability to zealously support an idea, and yet be open to change if new information comes along that supports a different viewpoint.

This is demonstrated literally by the book you hold in your hand at this moment. What the heck is a "good ol' boy" from Texas doing with a book about yoga?

Welcome to the 21st century! It's a time where we need trusted resources and rock-solid advice to move forward. We need great people to lead us. We need heroes and she-roes to follow.

This book and its recipe for recovering your emotional well-being could literally create a much-needed mental health revolution. It requires each of us to commit to DOING what is required, and that personal plan for each of us is laid out in this book.

I know you will enjoy and benefit from this heartfelt book and the caring man who's helping you on the road back to health.

Many blessings,

Barry Spilchuk

Table of **Contents**

CHAPTER 1

Life in the A.S.A.P. Lane!

This Is a Life of Being
Anxious—Stressed—Addicted—Pressured

Who is driving this A.S.A.P.-ing mobile? It could be your spouse, your significant other, your partner, your boss, a neighbor, a colleague, or a family member. Ultimately, and honestly, *you* and *I* are creating all this A.S.A.P.-ing ourselves.

Have you noticed, either in yourself or in people who are close to you, that you or they are feeling more anxious lately? Maybe you are prone to have your fuse "go off" faster than usual. You're not alone. In the last three years, anxiety levels in America have risen faster than any other country (Unisys Security Index).

Our way of coping has made us into addicts without our realizing it. Opioids and alcohol are the popular choice to "relieve" our stress. You can add cookies, cakes, pies, chocolate, and sugar to the list of "acceptable" coping mechanisms. Acceptable, simply because sugar fixes are legal. They are dangerous, but legal. In 1990, no state in the United States had an obesity rate of 15 percent. Today, 44 states have an obesity rate over 25 percent! Also, add buying more "stuff" in this frantic effort to cope. It's called "retail therapy" for a reason.

If you have had the opportunity to visit a doctor lately, or if you have heard about what's going on in many doctor's offices, it's truly alarming. Many doctors have substituted prescriptions for prevention. Why? They're living and working in the A.S.A.P. Lane as well! They are overworked and stressed, like the rest of us. It's human nature to take the quick and the easy way out. Enter the pharmaceutical companies—and their fix-of-the-day plan.

If I may paraphrase Oscar Wilde, "Why is it that no one ever told me that in one single tiny cell, we could hold both God's heaven and God's hell?"

> **More Americans will die this year from opioid overdoses than the combined total of the wars in Vietnam, Afghanistan, and Iraq.**

The pill-pushing companies have done a few "heavenly" things as they have invented some miracle medications that truly do solve problems for the masses. The "hellish" part comes from their desire to fix everything with a pill. Of course, profits drive them but even they have to admit that there is not a pill for every problem. Nor should there be.

False Wizards and Deaths of Despair

No matter how old you are, you probably know someone who has served in the military. They have *voluntarily* (in most cases) put on a uniform and said, "I've got your back. Not on my watch!" We owe each and every one of our military personnel and their families a *forever* debt of gratitude. We lost a lot of very good souls in Vietnam over ten years, and lost many more in the continuing conflicts in Afghanistan and Iraq. Here's an unbelievable fact: More Americans will die this year from opioid overdoses than the combined total of the wars in Vietnam, Afghanistan, and Iraq.

These "deaths of despair" are occurring at record rates, touching virtually every community in our country. We *voluntarily* (in most cases) pop pills in desperate hope of finding temporary "peace".

Opioid overdoses are now the leading cause of death for those under 50. I choose to call opioids "false wizards" simply because they give "false hope" like the Wizard of Oz did to those who ingest them. We hope that the pill can overtake the will—the will to do what's necessary to really heal.

These false wizards are dangerous even when they are not fatal. Simply put, they are destructive to our health, well-being, and happiness.

The Ebony Smith Story

She is the self-titled Ghetto Guru, founder of Yoga N Da Hood, a certified yoga instructor, and trailblazing leader in bringing yoga and meditation to those in great need but with little exposure or ability to attend formal yoga classes. Her inspiring story will  inspire anyone looking to ditch the false wizards and chart a new path to a better and healthier life. She was molested by women in her neighborhood at an early age. Traumatized by this, she became a "problem child". At school, she was frequently suspended, and was labeled a "bad kid". She turned to alcohol and attempted suicide twice in her twenties. During her first pregnancy at age 29, she was introduced to yoga by her doctor. "My soul was awakened, and my heart started to heal. For the first time, I discovered who I was and who I could become."

Yoga has changed Ebony's life, like it has changed the lives of so many other people. In addition to her regular yoga teaching, she offers free classes as outreach to her own community. She has created a nonprofit organization called Yoga N Da Hood, and there is more on her and her activities in the chapter on Yoga Evangelism (chapter 9).

The false wizards are extremely tricky, too. They lure us into a state of momentary happiness by enticing us with the age old come-ons like the following:

- Oh, go ahead, you deserve it.
- Just try it once—don't be a chicken.
- I'll eat just one more piece of cake.
- I'll smoke just one more cigarette.
- I just need this one more fix—I'll stop tomorrow.
- I'll go shopping just one more time. I need some me time.
- I'm happy—let's eat! I'm sad—let's eat!

Ultimately, just like the Wizard of Oz, each "word from the wizards" leads us to feel empty, sorrowful, disappointed, and increasingly addicted.

The stress that has overtaken our youth is at unprecedentedly high levels. Men and women of all ages are experiencing thinning hair, upset stomachs, and abnormal digestive issues.

We have also developed a "drunken monkey brain" just by our mental habits and practices. Like a monkey in the forest swinging from branch to branch, our anxiousness has caused our minds to jump from limb to limb in the forest of our minds. We ruminate about past mistakes. We hold on to regrets and grudges. We refuse to forgive ourselves or others for events long past. We are constantly worried about a "tomorrow" that, truthfully, never comes.

How our brain processes daily life, creates joy or anxiety. Negative and traumatic events get hardwired into our brains as emotional "knots". or toxins, just as our muscles, joints, and ligaments can develop physical "knots". This "hardwiring", increasingly toxic, covers all ages, both sexes, and cuts across all racial and ethnic groups. The healing power of yoga can be found on the Yellow Brick Road—in your *breath*! What's really good news is that we are born with "feel good" chemicals in our bodies (more on this in later chapters). Our brain has four natural chemicals ,that are stimulated, activated, and dispersed throughout our bodies during and after a yoga session. So say "goodbye" to the pills, chemicals, and false wizards. Say "goodbye" to the tsunami of stresses and anxieties that have overtaken your system. Say "goodbye" to your life in the A.S.A.P. Lane.

Say "hello" to a calmer, less anxious, healthier you. Say "hello" to your old chemical-free self. Say "hello" to the rest of your life being the best of your life.

Karl Marx, the Wizard, and the Yellow Brick Road

You might ask what possible connection there could be between this current mental health crisis, Karl Marx, yoga, and a fantasy book written over 100 years ago for children. Hardly a child grows up in America without reading the story or seeing the movie *The Wonderful Wizard of Oz*. Dorothy, her little dog Toto, the Scarecrow, the Tin Man, the Cowardly Lion, the Yellow Brick Road, the Wizard, the Emerald City, and the magical land of Oz are all etched as lasting memories for each of us. The Karl Marx connection will become evident in the next chapter.

Is this your life?

In my own practice of yoga, and in my teaching of others, I have come to use the story of the Emerald City as that place to which we all aspire—the "calm mind". It was over the rainbow where your troubles melted away and your dreams really did come true.

In the story, the Emerald City was only reachable by taking the Yellow Brick Road, and there lived the Wizard who would use his magical powers to help Dorothy and Toto get back to Kansas, get the scarecrow his much-desired brain, the Tin Man his heart and oil for his rusty joints, and the Cowardly Lion his courage.

Inspiring a Mass "Calm the Mind" Movement

We will see later how the path to the Emerald City (peace of mind) is through the breath (Yellow Brick Road), and mindful movement (yoga). Ultimately, the "wizards" we use to try to reach a state of happiness, like the Wizard of Oz, turn out to be false wizards, leaving us feeling empty, disappointed, and increasingly addicted.

This book has the very modest ambition of inspiring a mass movement among those who are today much in need of, yet not actively participating in any organized and systematic way of self-management or self-regulation of this tsunami of stress and anxiety that grip many today.

As more and more of us have discovered the empty promise of the false wizards, yoga's popularity has soared in recent years. It is an ancient tradition, rooted in more than 3,000 years of practice and tradition, yet it didn't get to the West until the late 19th century.

The 2016 "Yoga in America Study" conducted by *Yoga Journal* and the Yoga Alliance report that the number of practitioners in the United States has almost doubled over the past 5 years, from 20.4 million to almost 37 million; while spending on classes, equipment, clothing, and accessories rose from $10.7 to $16 billion over the same period. There are an estimated 76,000 certified yoga instructors, 65 percent do yoga at home, and almost 40 percent are fifty years old or older (American Association of Retired People).

Much of this growth is driven by the continuing search among those who are the most fitness- and health-conscious for better health, more flexibility, balance, strength, and ultimately the lifelong search for the "calm mind". I expect the growth trend to continue among that segment of the population.

This book, however, is focused on those most urgently in need and, yet, who are not included today. The vast majority of people still rely on the false wizards or just struggle through to cope with the stresses of the "bigger, better, faster and more" demands of life today.

CHAPTER 2

The Future Is NOW and It SUCKS... But It Doesn't Have To!

I s the future literally pinning your ears back because it's getting here so fast? *Future Shock*, an international bestseller written by Alvin Toffler in 1970, saw, even that long ago, society moving rapidly to "a hyper-condition of distress and psychological disturbance brought on by a person's inability to cope with rapid social, economic and technological change".

Yes, you say, how simple and slow life must have been in the 1970's without PDAs (personal digital assistants), the Internet, social media, or video games. For the younger reader, believe me, it was a long way from "simple and slow"! Yet in those days the only contact people had with technology and computers was through utility bills, bank and payroll services, and computer-generated junk mail.

Our constant companions—our cellphones—and all the other devices, apps, and social media tools that serve as our pit crew for life in the A.S.A.P. Lane were still years away. The digital revolution, with its many advantages and its negative economic-dislocation consequences, was seemingly still in the *distant* future.

Jobs assembling cars, television sets, or air conditioners, for example, seemed secure, providing a stable future and the ability to realize the proverbial American Dream. The World Trade Organization, North American Free Trade Agreement (NAFTA), and other agreements that took away protection from foreign competition, and hence jobs, were still 20 years away.

Talk radio and television, an industry that today thrives and prospers through keeping us in a constant state of alarm, worry, and anger at "the other side" was still fifteen years in the future.

Are you in fear of your job being made obsolete by a robot or some other rapidly advancing new technology? To you, this is "stone-cold" destruction! Yet, economists call this *creative destruction*. It is an economic concept first enunciated by Karl Marx, the father of socialism, and later refined by the Austrian economist Joseph Schumpeter. He called it a "gale of creative destruction". which revolutionizes the economic structure from within, "incessantly destroying the old one and creating a new one". This term is meant to describe the ongoing process within a free-market system where innovation and technological advances are in a never-ending state of creating new wealth and lifestyle advances to the benefit of the greatest number.

If you're thinking, "I ain't the greatest number, I'm me, and I can't keep up!" you are not alone. This feeling of being left behind is driving much of the destructive personal behavior and reliance on false wizards to help cope that is seen today.

While it is true that large segments of society have benefited from all the technological advances and trade deals of the past several decades, the social cost, which continues to climb, has been enormous. Forty-seven years since *Future Shock* appeared, the social cost has reached tsunami proportions, and the toll on those who can't adapt to the pace is becoming fatal in an alarmingly high number of cases, and immobilizing in many others.

> If you're thinking, "I ain't the greatest number, I'm me, and I can't keep up!" you are not alone. This feeling of being left behind is driving much of the destructive personal behavior and reliance on false wizards to help cope that is seen today.

This crisis isn't sparing your lawyer or your doctor either, who face unrelenting pressures to perform and may also be relying on a chemical crutch to get through their day. Alcohol and drug abuse among doctors is well chronicled, and is partly responsible for the high rate of preventable deaths and readmissions to hospitals. A recent study done by the Hazelden Betty Ford Foundation and the American Bar Association found an alarmingly high use of both alcohol and opioids among attorneys.

Brian Cuban, author of *The Addicted Lawyer: Tales of the Bar, Booze, Blow, and Redemption*, was recently quoted in a *New York Times* article entitled "The Lawyer, the Addict" on addiction in the legal profession: "I would regularly show up for work drunk and do a few lines of coke in the bathroom to recover from a hangover. Cocaine got me back on focus."

If we're looking for an economics weatherman to calm our anxiety by telling us that this "gale of destruction" will abate or slow down, it's very hard to find one. Microchips and robots will make this an ongoing problem. Mark Zuckerberg, CEO of Facebook, told the Harvard University class of 2017 that, "increased automation would strip us of our jobs and our purpose."

The promise in yoga and meditation is not in changing these external events, but in equipping you to more calmly process them and take constructive steps. After you've done something stupid, like shoot someone the "one finger Boy Scout salute" when they cut you off in traffic, and almost get run off the road when they retaliate, do you ever wonder how you could have lost control and perhaps become another gunshot casualty? This is an increasingly common occurrence in our major cities.

Bigger, Better, Faster, Stronger—Mind Turbulence!

In chapter 7 (Monkeys Are Cute... Unless They Are in Your Head), I discuss how your brain floods your prefrontal cortex with cortisol and immobilizes your process of making rational choices. The irrational choice in many cases becomes a life-threatening one. It can be like the road-rage example above or like finding a way to deaden the pain from any of a number of personal traumas or significant stress-related incidents.

Stress is a killer, and is taking its toll in a myriad of ways: "deaths of despair", alcoholism, obesity, heart disease, and diabetes.

"Bigger, better, faster, stronger", has always been a national American mantra and a personal one for many individuals.. The essence of free market democracies and economics is Darwinian—survival of the fittest. What is new is the pace at which one must see, process, and absorb all the factors that are necessary for informed, rational decision-making. The impact of this is simply too much for many young and older people to handle, and they are coping in various self-destructive ways.

Does "mind turbulence" resonate with you as a good way to describe your daily life? Do you find worry, anxiety, and depression to be your ever-present companions? In extreme cases, it is more than turbulence, and it becomes trauma.

Today's gale of destruction, like the cyclone that swept up Dorothy and Toto on the Kansas plains and deposited them in a strange yet magical place called Oz, is sweeping up increasingly large numbers of people and depositing them not in magical places but in strange and terrifying places.

CHAPTER 3

How Do I Get My Health Back? Just Follow the Yellow Brick Road

Are you telling me that there is an exit ramp off this A.S.A.P. Lane I'm on?

YES, I am telling you that! The Yellow Brick Road—your breath, given to you by God the day you were born, is your path to the Emerald City, a calm and stable mind. Dorothy was told to stay on the path, for there was "country that is dark and terrible" if she strayed. She was cautioned about wicked witches and other frightening beings and creatures. Any one or all of the addictions that have become your coping crutches are witches and goblins in their own right, and don't just exist in a fantasy book. They are your daily reality, in your mind, where your thoughts and emotions reside, robbing your life of its vitality and throttling your dreams.

Lucy's Moment of Truth

If you are a trauma victim, mind turbulence can be like the tornado that picked up Dorothy and Toto and took them to that distant and mysterious Land of Oz, leaving mind and brain wreckage in its wake and a "country that is dark and terrible" to navigate. The trauma victim lives each day on the edge of irrational and sometimes violent responses to imagined provocations.

If you, like the vast majority of people who are otherwise physically healthy but must sometimes deal with the overwhelming pressures of job, family, finances, and so on, take the Yellow Brick Road exit off the A.S.A.P. Lane. You can now head off much bigger problems later in life. The vagus nerve network, described and explained in the next chapter, is at work every moment of our lives, distributing every emotion, thought, and reaction to stress throughout every single organ of our body.

> **If you, like the vast majority of people who are otherwise physically healthy but must sometimes deal with the overwhelming pressures of job, family, finances, and so on, take the Yellow Brick Road exit off the A.S.A.P. Lane, you can now head off much bigger problems later in life.**

You may see yoga as primarily a difficult physical practice, made up of contorting poses or body positions, practiced by and appropriate for mostly young, athletic, hyperfit women. Take a second look at this, though, and you will see that men and women of all body types, ages, and races are saying, like Lucy, "I'm not willing to be miserable anymore!"

Like me, many of the current practitioners of yoga were originally drawn to the practice because of their dedication to actively "managing" their physical health. Years of running, weight training, and other forms of active fitness training create joint stiffness, and muscle tightness. Due to inheriting good genes and actively managing my health, I always got good reports on my annual physicals. But it has taken all of this time for me to finally realize that true "fitness" requires *mind* fitness as well, and that all the annual "high marks" I was getting were only half of the equation.

Want to burn the day's stresses and strains and leave them all in an ash heap? Yes, you will be able to touch your toes again, become stronger, and regain your balance, but the pinnacle of a yoga practice, on top of all these other benefits, is the *calming of the mind*!

> **The foundation of yoga, and the most important thing to master, is something we've all been doing since the day we were born—breathing!**

"If You Can Breathe, You Can Do Yoga"

The foundation of yoga, and the most important thing to master, is something we've all been doing since the day we were born—breathing!

You may be wondering, how you can breathe any differently than you already do? Most of us react to stress by shallow breathing. Simply defined, *mindful breathing* is inhaling deeply through the nose, up from your diaphragm, pausing at the top for three to four seconds, and exhaling through the nose, all the way to the bottom, and pausing again at the bottom. Repeating this rhythmic process while participating in a yoga session, or as part of a 20-minute meditation session practiced on a consistent basis, is the true path to "peace of mind". (See the next pages for several techniques.)

Getting to "now" and remaining in the now standard time (NST) zone requires managing a consistent rhythm in your breathing. Most of us breathe from the chest, and the shallow breath signals to the brain that we are stressed.

How often do you say or think, "I just want to be happy!" The state of "happiness"—a mind free of anxiety, worry, and stress—is one we pursue throughout our lives. The secret to this, one can find, like the Scarecrow, the Tin Man, and the Cowardly Lion, lies within. Furthermore, it is readily accessible through life's greatest gift—the breath, the Yellow Brick Road. Stay on it... the Emerald City is very near.

Man, if I hadn't learned how to take a deep breath, do you think I could sit here and watch this mangy skunk eat my food?

Just as Dorothy was cautioned about the hostile territory through which she would have to walk, you as a rhythmic breather will also find distractions in the form of "mind chatter" that will challenge your ability to stay on the path. Our thoughts, emotions, and fears are constant topics of silent conversation in our minds, and a constant barrier to mind peace. Like everything else, "managing the monkey" becomes much easier through following a disciplined practice.

Mindful Breathing Techniques

Breathing options and techniques (see appendix for more on these):

- **Darth Vader Breath**: also, called ocean breath. I find this technique the most effective, and there are several ways of doing it. My preferred way is to curl my tongue up to the roof of the mouth, inhale through the nose, up deeply from the pelvic floor, up through the diaphragm, pausing three to four seconds at the top, visualize a small hole in the throat, and exhale slowly, but resolutely, making the Darth Vader noise or ocean sound out the imagined hole in the throat.

- **Taco:** This technique is especially effective in cooling the body and brain after a vigorous, sweaty workout or power yoga session. Curl the tongue, like a taco, and inhale deeply through the mouth, holding for a count of two to three seconds and then exhale through the nose.
- **Alternate Nostril Method:** This technique is better utilized as part of a meditation session or at the opening of a yoga session, as it requires using the hands to manipulate the nostrils alternately, and this is difficult during an active yoga session as the arms and hands are very active during a standard session.
- **Left Nostril Breathing:** Find a comfortable seated position. Block your right nostril with right index finger, close your eyes, relax your jaw and brow, inhale deeply and long, pause at the top for three to four seconds, then exhale long and slowly through the left nostril. On the inhale, you might add silently the word "letting" and on the exhale, "go". Continue for three to five minutes.
- **Bellows Breath:** This technique is particularly effective for "jump-starting" a yoga session, as it is a quick energizer, consisting of deep inhales, followed by fast, vigorous exhales. A set of three of these, followed by reverting to the Darth Vader method, is good for mid-afternoon or after-work sessions, when energy may be lagging.

The challenge to "breathe mindfully" becomes an even bigger challenge when you try to synchronize your breathing with a consistent set of yoga poses as you go through a session. Don't fret over the "wandering" but just gently acknowledge the thought and come back to your breath. You will find the effort and patience worth the time invested.

CHAPTER 4

In the Jungle... the Lion Sleeps Tonight! But What If He CAN'T?

---✸---

"My body aches, my mind races, and my soul feels empty. I still have dreams, but right now, I would settle for a good night's sleep."

---✸---

As you confront the A.S.A.P.'s in your life and find that coping is becoming more and more difficult, are you looking for wizards and finding that you get relief, but only temporarily, from another pill, another shot of vodka, another cookie, or another session of retail therapy?

In the story, as Dorothy started her trek along the Yellow Brick Road, she began to encounter others with a need to see the Wizard, whom they believed possessed the magical powers to grant their greatest wishes and make their dreams come true. First, there was the Scarecrow, who wanted a "brain" with which to think and make wise choices. Dorothy's entourage grew as they trekked along and encountered the Tin Man, who desired two things: A heart with which to love, and oil for his joints, which grew rusty each time it rained. Finally, as their destination grew closer, the group, full of hope, encountered what they thought was the most fearsome creature in the forest—a Lion, the King of the Jungle. When they recoiled in horror, he quickly said, "Don't be afraid. I know I'm supposed to be King of the Jungle, but I'm afraid, I'm a coward, and I need courage."

For you, yoga and meditation in the real world will indeed provide oil for the joints (flexibility and strength), a calmer brain with which to make "wiser" choices, and "courage" by clearing your mind of the chatter and clutter, which hinders us from pursuing our dreams to "go for it." When the mind is blinded by fear and mind chatter, the eyes cannot see.

When the mind is blinded by fear and mind chatter, the eyes cannot see.

Did you know that there is a direct link between our thoughts, emotions, feelings, and the physical impact on our physical body and organs? If your heart, lungs, liver, and other vital organs are getting a constant transmission from your brain of stress, anxiety, and depression, the physical toll over time can be enormous and lead to premature aging and early death.

Don't Skip this Part, or Let Your Eyes Glaze Over!

This can be the difference between vibrant health and so much of what ails all of us, both physically and mentally. Suffice to say, it can become a matter of life and death, and it is, in fact, becoming a matter of "death" for many.

Dr. Melanie Greenberg, Ph.D.

Fix your brain—fix your life!

The *Stress-Proof Brain* is more than a book that explains your brain and how it functions. It includes many practical tools to perform self-analysis and self-treatment. It can help you "rewire" your stress response to be more flexible, positive, and wise.

You should buy this book. Here are some highlights:

- "Many addictive behaviors such as drinking, smoking, taking drugs, overeating, and overindulging in shopping or sex are, at their root, attempts to avoid the uncomfortable emotions from stress."

- "Emotional eating is directly linked to cortisol levels and stress."
- "Studies show that persons under chronic stress can age prematurely, up to ten years sooner than peers."
- "Mindfulness has the potential to make not only individuals, but businesses, institutions and societies stress-proof."
- "Your breath is the most common anchor in learning and adopting mindfulness into your life."
- "Adult brains can be rewired through a process called neuroplasticity."
- "Mindfulness, practiced 30 minutes per day, can actually shrink your amygdala."
- "You can become the CEO of your own brain, keep your prefrontal cortex firmly in charge, and make your brain less reactive to stress."
- "You can generate inner calm, build healthy lifestyle habits, and facilitate clear thinking."
- "A stress-resilient brain is the best thing you can have for staying focused, fit, connected, and on top of your game.
- Dr. Greenberg says, "If I had to choose one tool, it would be mindfulness."

You may see this as "going into the weeds" to start examining this connection and how all the body organs connect to and are impacted by our thoughts, beliefs, and emotions. To you and those earnestly searching for answers, such as:

- A mother or father of a son or daughter who overdosed, who are haunted by "where did we go wrong?"
- Someone, in a sober moment, asking, "How did my life go off the rails this way?"

- Others who make moral judgments, on the basis of thinking it just comes from not being taught what's right at home and
- You, like Lucy, saying, "'This is bullshit,' I'm taking my life back."

To all of you, what follows will help you understand how our brain and mind can lead us astray, and how to get it back on the Yellow Brick Road and on the path to the Emerald City.

Air-Traffic Control: The Prefrontal Cortex

To fully understand how and why "false wizards" become the default choice for many of us, it is necessary to understand something that most of us have never heard about or given any attention to. The prefrontal cortex, like air traffic control, is that part of the brain that lies just behind our forehead. As our eyes and ears take in the sights and sounds around us, we process with the prefrontal cortex what we see and hear, our thoughts about it, and weigh the consequences and make considered decisions on next steps.

Have you wondered, "Why do I lose it sometimes for even the slightest provocation, or why did I react to that idiot on the expressway the other day, who cut in front of me? What if he had a gun?

The Hijacker: The Amygdala

The amygdala, located near the center of our brain, is part of our "threat system". Its job is to keep us safe by alerting us to danger. It is the brain's "emotional" computer, unlike the prefrontal cortex, which is the logical computer. Unfortunately, it isn't very good at discriminating between real dangers "out there" and dangers we are just thinking about. It elicits the same response in both cases, and can even be set off even by an unpleasant memory from the past, even though the danger has passed.

If you are a trauma survivor, the "false trigger" is particularly problematic in extreme cases where trauma has occurred. The prefrontal cortex, where calm, rational weighing of risk and reward takes place, can get "hijacked" and become flooded with cortisol. A recent case in point is that of Chris Kyle, a much-decorated U.S. Navy Seal from the war in Iraq. Kyle wanted to be of help to a fellow veteran and had taken him to a shooting range in Texas as an act of charity. However, he was killed by that fellow veteran, who was suffering from a severe case of PTSD. It was never determined what the trigger was in this case, and it is one of many recent cases where a returning veteran, traumatized by their service in one of our recent wars, has committed some inexplicable act of violence.

The encouraging news is that yoga and meditation are proving to be very effective in helping trauma survivors, including more serious cases of PTSD (see Chapter 8).

Sedating the Monkey!

Your "monkey"—and we all have one—resides in our prefrontal cortex most of the time and creates all the back-and-forth chatter as we go about our busy daily lives. While the chatter is distracting and robs our days of much of the joy and satisfaction we would otherwise enjoy, it doesn't become dangerous until the monkey gets scared by some event or trigger, and then jumps back to the amygdala and "starts screeching at the top of its voice".

Even among otherwise emotionally healthy persons, incidents like road rage or a perceived insult in a social setting can set off a "hijacking" of the prefrontal cortex by the amygdala, meaning a flood of cortisol has occurred and the person will act in some rash way, possibly with tragic consequences.

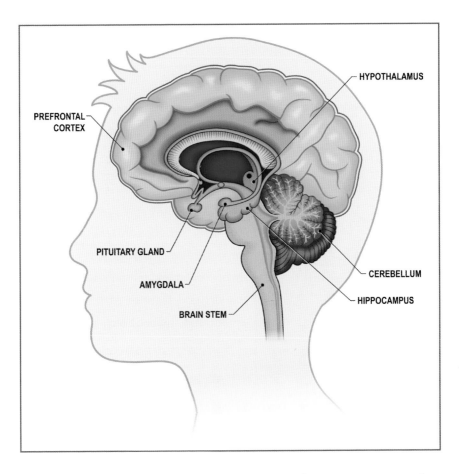

Are you a doubter about all the hype you hear from we yoga evangelists on its healing powers? (More on yoga evangelism in Chapter 10.)

Stayed tuned in, and don't skip to the next chapter! I can hear some of you now, saying, "Man, this is getting deep, and do I really need to know this stuff with all the unpronounceable names?"

Here's the Yoga Magic!

Mentioned briefly in a preceding chapter, is not Las Vegas, but *vagus* (pronounced the same), and it is the *most important nerve in your body*! It is your body's interstate highway system or road network, and is the key to understanding the magic of yoga, the feeling of calm, hydration, radiance,

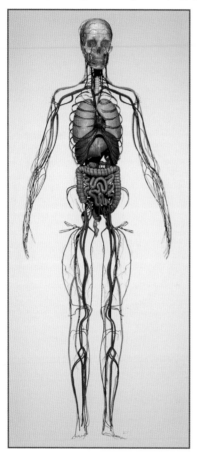

or even bliss that one experiences during and after a vigorous yoga session.

It is also the way to understand the toll that anxiety can take on the rest of our internal organs. It is among the many complex, perplexing, and least understood features of the mysterious integrated human biological miracle: The human body.

As you can see from the illustration above, this nerve branches out from the brain and connects to all the vital organs, wending its way throughout the maze of the body's organs and viscera all the way to the colon. Constant stress tips the balance toward a "hijacking" by the amygdala, thus promoting inflammation, hypertension, anxiety, insomnia, obesity, and accelerated aging.

THE YOGA MAGIC!

Yoga stimulates the vagus nerve that carries information from the brain to all of the body's major organs. Most importantly, it also transmits those four natural "feel good" chemicals you were given at birth (serotonin, dopamine, oxytocin, endorphins), which calm and slow everything down and allow self-regulation.

News bulletin! Your happiness does depend on drugs. You've just been using the wrong ones! You have a pharmacy in your head! Use the ones given to you at birth.

Okay, one final big word: *Neuroplasticity*! The stimulation of the vagus nerve makes rewiring of the brain, possible. If you are a PTSD survivor, or if you have a family member or neighbor who has suffered a trauma of any sort, this is good and encouraging news! This is particularly important to people with more advanced cases, such as trauma survivors. It is a process "that makes it possible to healthily increase the size, strength and density of our brains, just like physical exercise can make our muscles stronger and denser with more endurance" (Consciousness Research Institute).

CHAPTER 5

My BFF: Downward-Facing Dog! Breathing My Way to the Emerald City

YOU are my target!

You, whose life is being blown and buffeted by this gale of change!

You, who have dreams and ambitions, but keep getting knocked down!

You, who hate your job!

You, who, like Lucy, are saying, I'm sick and tired of being sick and tired!

And all of you:

- Stressed-out schoolteachers or administrators
- Pre-K children from a stressful home environment
- Parents looking for a way to give your children tools to manage their lives in the most stressful time ever in our history for young people
- College students using binge-drinking to cope

- Men who think yoga is not masculine enough
- Overweight, out of shape men or women
- Already physically fit amateur or professional athletes
- Famous but insecure celebrities
- Stressed business executives
- Seniors going gently into that good night

Man's best friend forever: Downward-Facing Dog, the most famous pose in all of yoga (see Resources section), and, how ironic that an endearing little dog would play such a key role in The Wizard of Oz.

The target audience for this book is the person caught up in the swirl of "the gale of destruction" referenced in Chapter 2, and looking for a way to self-regulate their own response to their own "gale". This includes those using false wizards. It also includes the physically fit athlete, already familiar with the natural endorphin high, but who is still laboring under the illusion that physical strength and speed give them all the competitive edge they need.

Man's best friend forever: Downward-Facing Dog, the most famous pose in all of yoga (see Resources section), and, how ironic that an endearing little dog would play such a key role in The Wizard of Oz. Dorothy had Toto on her journey, and this pose, along with the others, is yours. Just like that proverbial "journey of a thousand miles beginning with the first step", your ditching the false wizards begins with that first "mindful breath".

Toto Finally Gets His Due

Toto and his role in one of our greatest and most inspiring fairy tales is finally getting his due—at least in this book, and increasingly elsewhere. Therapy dogs are playing important roles in treating trauma survivors along with a yoga and meditation regimen. Remember that it was Toto who finally pulled the curtain back, exposing the false wizard.

Lauren Walker, founder, Energy Medicine Yoga and bestselling author of *The Energy Medicine Yoga Prescription*:

"Animals transform us. They teach us about unconditional love. They teach us responsibility, trust, commitment. But they teach us much more than that. Animals often bring us into hidden areas of our own lives. They show us where to go, often leading us home. They find us when we're missing, they can tell us when we're going to be sick or fall down, and they can be our eyes, our ears, our senses. But even just a

Lauren and Louis

pet, just a pet, can change our lives. Animals have held a sacred role in the lives of humans as far back as history records. Animals hold a primal, intuitive wisdom connection to us. In Native American traditions, and Native wisdom everywhere, spirit animals guide us and their energy is called Medicine.

"It's no mistake that the pivotal turning point of the whole plotline of the film The Wizard of Oz was based on the dog. Toto embodies the trickster, the one who leads the protagonist down the road to her own wisdom and inner truths.

He starts her on her journey, and in the end, he is the one who reveals the hypocrisy that there is an external 'wizard' who might know more than we do.

"Animals have that capacity. To draw us along an otherwise hidden trajectory, into the wisdom and truth that always reside in our hearts. That first yoga pose."

If the pictures and illustrations look too hard, getting underway requires only being able to "breathe" and doing only what your body will allow. A caution you will hear from many instructors is "Go only to your limit, never past your limit." This frees you to only "be present", following your breath as you do each pose, being unconcerned about the person next to you or any peer pressure you may feel from others in class.

For you, the beginner, the good news is that doing the pose *correctly* isn't important.

As you progress, you will become more flexible, balanced, stronger, and overall, much healthier. These are all outcomes you can expect from starting this journey on the Yellow Brick Road. Your destination, the Emerald City—the calm mind—is reached through the combination of breathing and poses that activate those natural "feel-good" brain chemicals that travel from the brain throughout the entire vagus nerve network, discussed in the last chapter.

For you, the beginner, the good news is that doing the pose *correctly* isn't important. This is very important to note, as it is an excuse or reason often given by some who are afraid to try yoga, especially men.

Lauren Walker

Lauren Walker, named one of the 100 most influential yoga teachers in the United States, has been teaching yoga for 20 years. With her innovative merging of energy medicine and yoga, she turbocharges our pursuit of mind-body fitness.

To have the life you truly want and deserve, you have to heal the issues that are holding you back. Some of these are physical, some emotional, some spiritual—all are rooted in the energy flow through your body.

You owe it to yourself to understand how literally everything—body, mind, and spirit are connected and how the flow of energy through your body has the most profound impact on your overall well-being. The book you are reading, as I hope I have communicated, is focused on the person not practicing yoga or meditation today, yet, searching for a way to exit a life being overwhelmed by all the pressures of life in the A.S.A.P. Lane.

LAUREN WALKER

THE ENERGY MEDICINE YOGA PRESCRIPTION

Learn five core practices   Discover three essential habits   Activate your body's   Create a powerful new vision
for hundreds of ailments   for well-being   natural healing intelligence   for health and happiness

"I love these simple tools to help anyone get their energy working for them." SEANE CORN

A reviewer wrote, "Lauren's book will take your yoga practice—and your existence—out of the flatlands and into the majestic peaks."

My hope is that my book will persuade you to take the first step, and then know that Walker's book will take you to the next level.

You should get Lauren Walker's book. Here are some highlights:

- Energy is the underlying force of everything in the universe, and you can easily tap into the powerful energy systems in your own body.
- Once you know how to access this energy, you no longer row against your own internal flow.
- With a simple three-minute technique, you can harness this underlying energy and get it working for you (see the Wake Up three-minute sequence in her book).
- Your unprocessed emotions affect your health more than almost anything else, leading to stress and disease. Learn a daily EMYoga practice to help process your emotions.
- You can easily stimulate your immune system for greater health and vitality.
- Your core strength is different than you think. It's not six-pack abs. Learn a deeper way to truly strengthen both your physical core and your emotional core.
- Build joy and contentment with the practice of gratitude and directed journaling.
- Understand the power of sound to your health, and learn the most healing sounds you can utter.

For you, the beginner, and even for many more advanced practitioners, Vinyasa Flow (see Chapter 10), a version of Hatha, is probably the best from among the several different types of yoga available. This type of yoga seeks to unite the breath and the pose in one flowing movement, hence achieving an integrated benefit package of balance, strength, flexibility, health, and the ultimate achievement of the "calm mind".

As I mentioned before, I went to my first yoga session feeling that I needed more flexibility and balance, Yet I kept noticing body, mind, and brain effects that were different from the "endorphin highs" that I had always experienced with running and other aerobic activities. Believe me, like the legions worldwide who jog, run, or participate in other heart rate-elevating aerobic activities, I managed through two high-stress careers—politics and global business—by accessing those natural endorphins that got activated by a vigorous run.

With yoga and meditation, which also activate your endorphins, you also get the added bonus of healthy shots of dopamine, serotonin, and oxytocin. To this day, after a yoga session, my skin feels more alive—almost tingly—my knee-jerk responses to situations are fewer, my sleep deeper and better, and the list goes on...

For the new participant used to a vigorous regimen of aerobic and weight training, a Flow class can move through a one breath-one movement session at three seconds per breath-per movement pace and give you all the sweat, accelerated heart rate, and "burn" that you want. Likewise, it can move at a slower, gentler pace. In Chapter 10, you can find resource sites to see the different poses and a wide range of choices from which to choose.

CHAPTER 6

Can Anybody Find Me Some BODY to Love?

———— ✳ ————

"Sticks and stones may break my bones,
but words will never hurt me."

—Unknown

———— ✳ ————

We've all heard this old adage, probably for the first time around the sixth grade, and used it as a defense against something someone else has said about us. If you have a lot of self-confidence, maybe the words of others don't hurt. What's more damaging are those said by *us to us*, and by *us to others about us*!

Are you inviting the old man or old woman to move in—where your mind, spirit, and physical organs live?

- I can't do the things I used to be able to!
- OMG, my 30th birthday is next week, and I'm already feeling it!

- Look at my picture at the last high school reunion—what happened to me?
- Posting humorous "I'm getting old"-themed posts on Facebook.

Dr. Deepak Chopra, the leading authority on many things related to the mind–body connection, in his groundbreaking book *Ageless Body, Timeless Mind*, said that through our self-talk "We open the door and virtually throw a welcome party to the older version of ourselves, and in pretty short order, that's exactly who moves in and stays for the rest of our lives."

Deepak Chopra

- "Stress is the epidemic of our civilization."
- "Virtually all physical disease is connected to stress."
- "Stress is a perception of threat, real or imagined."
- "Sleep, meditation, yoga, nutrition are critical pillars of well-being."

Dr. Deepak Chopra and Author

Chopra's book had a profound effect on me, and those words still resonate almost 30 years later. I'm sure some of my good friends have long since gotten tired of my admonitions to stop the "old man's talk" when they would say something like the comments above.

As mentioned in the previous chapter, as the Tin Man, Dorothy, and Toto made their way along the Yellow Brick Road, the Tin Man said that he yearned for a new heart with which to love again, and oil for his rusty joints, which always became rusty after a rain.

Any yoga practitioner will quickly attest to the "oil for the joints" benefits that yoga brings. Most will also add "oil" for the spirit, body, and mind that yoga brings.

The Body Benefits

Due to the mental health crisis, the primary focus of this book so far has been about the impact that a dedicated yoga practice has on the mind and brain. In addition, most regular practitioners of a consistent and dedicated practice will discover a measurable, and in many cases, significant improvement in their physical health metrics (see below in this chapter). These benefits include slowing down premature aging.

I can remember during my early yoga sessions hearing the instructor read off a list of 75 positive health benefits, and thinking, "Yeah, yeah, yeah! Can we just get on with the stretching and flexibility poses so that I can touch my toes again?"

My Personal Health Story

Several years later, on top of the "mind benefits", my asthma is gone, I no longer require glasses, and every one of my eight key vital signs is within proper range, except for cholesterol HDL, which has improved but is still higher than considered optimal. Finally, the arthritis in my left hip, which used to require getting an injection every six months in order to continue my exercise regimen has largely disappeared. I have followed a disciplined fitness regimen for most of my life, so having only a "few issues" may be partly attributable to that, but, without question, a consistent regimen of yoga and daily meditation has contributed significantly to not only my excellent health, but also to my overall sense of well-being.

To be truly *fit* and *healthy* requires strength, flexibility, balance, and a *calm* mind. These are the rungs on the yoga benefits ladder. Gyms, running trails, and other "fitness clubs" are full of aerobically and muscularly fit disciplined men and women—with hyperactive "monkey brains". I know—I've been one of them! The endorphin high from these sessions is wonderful, and that kept me going back for more for all of my adult life, but, as I said before, the endorphins are only one of a part of a family of "feel-good" and calming natural brain chemicals that take you to a whole new level.

Mayo Clinic in its *Healthy Lifestyle* e-newsletter cited that:

The health benefits of yoga practice include:

- Stress reduction;
- Improved fitness; and
- Management of chronic conditions, including heart disease and high blood pressure.

Noteworthy physical benefits in addition:

- Fascia fitness - Along with the *vagus* nerve, the other big "Eureka!" for most people, even the otherwise physically fit, is the existence and importance of *fascia*, a band of tissue that surrounds our muscles, organs, bones, tendons, ligaments, and other structures of the body. Sometimes described as a "fascial suit", the most common analogy to explain or illustrate fascia is the white membrane that you see first when peeling an orange. "Fascia both connects and separates," and connects body parts at the same time.

- "Releasing fascial adhesions is like clearing out the cobwebs between muscles, allowing them to slide and glide more efficiently, which also increases hydration and release of toxins" (Allison Candelaria, *Yoga Journal*, June 2016).
- Flexibility - Oil for the joints, muscles, and fascia is a good way to think about flexibility and the improvements that one can expect from a disciplined yoga regimen.
- Balance - The natural balance that we all have as youth erodes over time, and this loss can lead to falls and serious injury later in life. Calming the mind and having improved joint and muscular flexibility both indirectly contribute to improved balance. There are also several poses or series of poses that directly target the improving of balance.
- Strengthening - Most of the poses contribute to a general toning and strengthening of the entire body. Especially effective are the Sun Salutation Series (A and B), which are both very good in building upper-body strength
- Psoas muscle and hip flexors - This muscle group is being singled out here for special attention, both because of its critical importance and the fact that it is, along with the vagus nerve, the least known and least understood. Technically, it isn't a hip flexor, even though it is often referred to as such. It is, arguably, the most important muscle in the body. The emotional knots or emotional toxins that get stored in the body, most often end up in the hips. The Psoas has been referred to as "the warehouse for the body's fear and trauma".

CHAPTER 7

Monkeys Are Cute... Unless They're in Your Head!

By now, you may be thinking, "This sounds interesting enough for me to try. My monkey seems to never sleep, wakes me up in the middle of the night, and also works a seven-day week... anything to calm him down! Yet, how can I commit to something I've never tried, and that looks difficult to me?"

---※---

"The mind is restless, unsteady, turbulent, wild, stubborn; truly, it seems to me as hard to master as the wind."

—*Bhagavad Gita 6.34*

---※---

Please be assured that even the most committed yoga practitioner has difficulty maintaining a full seven-day week of dedicated yoga sessions. With any form of physical exercise, the body requires rest and recovery time. While he's "leaping from limb to limb" in my mind with ruminations about my past, and worries about my future, how do I keep him calm between yoga sessions?

As discussed previously, the purpose of this book is to attract a new demographic to the practice of yoga, for the ultimate purpose of helping people calm this epidemic of anxiety, depression, and other forms of increasingly fatal means of succumbing to the "gale". Yoga is a workout, for sure, and in its complete form is movement, breath—and *meditation*.

———————— ✳ ————————

"Your mind will believe everything you tell it.
Feed it hope.
Feed it truth.
Feed it with love."

—Author Unknown

———————— ✳ ————————

In Chapter 9, a "how to get started" personal regimen is outlined, with options depending on your physical condition and appetite for a "toe in the water first, or a full jump into the deep water".

For the "deep water" person, it is suggested to practice yoga 3 times a week, and to meditate for 15–20 minutes each day. This keeps the focus on the Yellow Brick Road (mindful breathing) and the Emerald City (calm mind). A "toe in the water" approach could start out with a daily meditation regimen graduating to include yoga at a later time.

Now Standard Time

In the meantime, let me introduce you to yoga's first cousin, if not twin sibling: *Meditation!*

In the present moment, there is no Daylight Savings Time, Greenwich Mean Time, or any other time zone—only *now*! It's difficult to avoid clichés when writing or speaking about this, but clichés become clichés because of the truths embedded in them. "Yesterday is a memory, and tomorrow only a promise" is one of the more common ones.

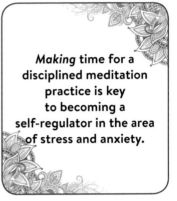

Making time for a disciplined meditation practice is key to becoming a self-regulator in the area of stress and anxiety.

"All man's miseries derive from not being able to sit quietly in a room alone."

—*Blaise Pascal*

Making time for a disciplined meditation practice is key to becoming a self-regulator in the area of stress and anxiety. The time we spend sitting in a quiet place, without distractions, for 20 minutes or so each day is not only about that short space of time during your day but also about becoming mindful throughout all parts of your life. Ruminating about past negative experiences or incessant worrying about future events keeps our judgment clouded with self-doubt, makes us risk-averse, and closes our hearts and minds to new experiences that could offer a relaunch in our lives. Rise, Pee, and Meditate (RPM)! This regimen, developed by Davidjij, is an easy and excellent way to make meditation a permanent, lasting, and healing ritual in your life.

Brain Performance Institute University of Texas at Dallas

- Breathing deeply stimulates the vagus nerve, which is the longest cranial nerve in the body. The vagus nerve activates the "relax and unwind" system in the brain.

(Left) Dianna Purvis Jaffin, Ph.D., PMP, Director, Strategy and Programs and (Right) Jenny Wright Howland, PsyD, Stress Solutions Program Manager

- Meditation benefits include increasing the "feel-good" chemicals in the brain, such as serotonin, dopamine, endorphins and oxytocin.

- Excess stress, experienced over a long period of time, causes a release of too much cortisol and can lead to many chronic health conditions.

The "wandering mind" is always present even with the experienced meditator. The beginner will sometimes throw their hands up after a few sessions and just say, "I can't do this!" As discussed in the chapter on breathing, there are techniques to manage the wandering mind better and help stay in the moment.

The Darth Vader breath or ocean breath is one of several breathing techniques that can be used. The objective is not to empty your mind but to "settle it into silence" and observe the thoughts and musings as they come and recognize them for what they are—just passing thoughts that come and go like butterflies or soft, drifting, wispy clouds.

Please forgive another cliché... but practice does make perfect (see Chapter 9 on a 66-day commitment), or at least makes us much better at anything we want to do. Practice will bring you closer and closer to a personal way of being able to observe and acknowledge the "distractions" and more easily let them pass for what they are—not reality but just ruminations.

As you progress and become more comfortable and less self-conscious, you will find yourself using meditation and breathing techniques in locations that before would have been too distracting, like airports, shopping malls, and so on.

In fact, I am now able to go through a vigorous, fast-paced Power Yoga session, complete with a loud, fast-music playlist, and never be distracted from my Darth Vader breathing rhythm. As I said before, I find this breathing method to be the best for keeping the monkey brain in check while in either a yoga or a meditation session. Life

The objective is not to empty your mind but to "settle it into silence".

is fast and often chaotic, so being able to slow things down and keep the prefrontal cortex in charge becomes key to both mental and physical health, and personal safety.

How to Do It

As this book is focused on the new convert, here are some principles for an effective meditation session (see Chapter 10 for ways to access "how to do it" illustrations and videos).

- First and foremost, fret not when you find it difficult at the start to stay focused. As stated, keeping yourself focused on breathing is a challenge for even the most experienced practitioner of yoga. As with the poses, it is common for the beginner to wonder, "Am I doing it right?" The good news is that "your way is the right way".

- Take a seat: Beginners often feel strange sitting cross-legged on the ground. In addition, at first it can also be painful to sit that way. I sit cross-legged on my mat, without any other support. However, for my daily meditation sessions at home, I use a sofa cushion, which I return to the sofa when finished.

- For the beginner, sitting in a chair or against the wall may be a good starting point, as the objective is not to master an unfamiliar, and possible painful, sitting position but to use mindful breathing to calm the wandering mind. When choosing this method, do remember to sit away from the back of the chair, and place your feet firmly on the floor, aligned with your hips and knees.

- Sit tall with an elongated spine and shoulders back. For those whose work requires sitting all day, slumping shoulders become a default position throughout the days and weeks, leading to posture issues, aches, and pains. Beginning your daily meditation session this way, and making it a daily practice, can start you on the road back to more upright posture and fewer neck, shoulder, and back issues.

- Resting the hands: The more experienced practitioner will usually be seen employing the "hands resting on knees, index finger and thumb touching" technique. However, for the beginner, there are several ways, and all of them suitable: Resting the hands comfortably in your lap, one cupped in the other; hands on knees with palms resting up; or left hand over belly-button and right hand over heart.

- Relaxing the brow, shoulders, and jaw: As you start your meditation session, closing your eyes, sitting quietly and visualizing a full body scan is a good way to harness your focus right at the start. Bringing your focus to your brow, then slowly moving through a visualization exercise that moves down through your eyes, sinuses, jaw, and shoulders, is a good way to achieve this right at the start. I have found myself halfway through a 20-minute session, only to suddenly become aware of a tight jaw and brow, so I have adopted the "body scan" approach in order to obviate this.

It is the journey, not the destination.

- The walking or "moving" meditation: Aside from what most meditators use—the "sitting" method, another useful method, especially for the highly stressed streets of major cities where people walk to and from work, is walking slowly and consciously focusing on each step and each breath.

This requires adopting an entirely new personal mantra: "It is the journey, not the destination" that matters.

Adopting this new attitude is no small undertaking, because the major streets, avenues, and boulevards of the world's larger cities are full of pedestrians on a mission: "Take no prisoners" in getting to my destination in the shortest possible time, without making eye contact or saying hello! Again, the mantra must become "It is the journey, not the destination".

My Manhattan Island Walking Meditation Experience

To share a personal example, after 9/11, "We Are All New Yorkers" was used widely as a means of showing solidarity and empathy with the people of New York. As I reflected on my own experience of New York City, I realized that after 40-plus years of fairly frequent trips and visits, my "New York World" was that mostly between 42nd Street and 57th Street—Midtown.

I decided to take an entire day and walk the entire length of Manhattan Island, in order to truly experience the neighborhoods and ethnic diversity of this most famous of the city's five boroughs. I started at 6:30 a.m. at Battery Park on the very southern tip of Manhattan and ended at 7:30 p.m. that evening in Marble Hill, the northernmost neighborhood of the island—a distance of 14 miles.

I started with no chosen route or targeted end time, only with the aim of mindfully wending my way through the various neighborhoods that make up one of the world's most ethnically diverse cities. Those famous words of the poet Emma Lazarus from the Statue of Liberty, "Bring me your huddled masses yearning to be free" reverberated in my ears as I made my way up through Wall Street, Tribeca, Chinatown, SoHo, Little Italy, Greenwich Village, and through Midtown to 57th Street, where Central Park begins.

Walking with no set end time and no particular destination in mind other than the northern end of the island, I was experiencing this great city in a way I never had before. It took another six hours to move through Spanish Harlem, Harlem, Hamilton Heights, Washington Heights, Fort George, and into Inwood, where I was able to hail a cab and ride back to my midtown hotel.

It is said that it is "better to travel first-class than to arrive". Experiencing each moment, taking each step, making eye contact with people who don't look like you and maybe don't even speak your language is like that—a truly first-class way to go.

To conclude this chapter on meditation, in the *Yoga Sutra*, Patanjali underlines the life lesson that is at the center of this book:

"Meditation begins when we discover that our never-ending quest to possess things and our continual craving for pleasure and security can never be satisfied. When we finally realize this, our external quest turns inward."

The false wizards are with us always, seeking and often succeeding in keeping our attention focused outward on things that are not only "false" but also destructive to our health and well-being.

CHAPTER 8

The Ultimate Yoga Machine: BMW (Breathe—Move—Wonder)!

Casey Williams is the True Embodiment of Wonder Woman (see full profile later along with two other Wonder Woman profiles).

" I had never really thought about yoga. There is a stigma in my community that it's for rich people who walk around with iced coffee and live with dogs! I have never really seen any African Americans practice yoga or even heard of any in my community."

Casey is a 36-year-old woman from Dallas, raised by a single mother, and married with three daughters, namely her twins Kaitlynn and Courtlynn, age 10, and a younger daughter, Kamryn. Like many women who not only have a professional career, but also hands on in her family and a responsible parent, Casey is dealing with all the stress and pressure that go with that (see full profile on page 62).

Are you one of those people who think: "No one like me does yoga,"... or these?

- A Pre-K to high-school-senior student
- A teacher
- A college student
- A man who thinks yoga is not masculine enough
- Wonder Woman—stressed to the max
- An overweight, out-of-shape man or woman
- A trauma survivor with PTSD
- An already "fit" amateur or professional athlete
- A celebrity
- A business executive
- A senior "going gently into that good night"

With nearly 40 million Americans practicing yoga, and that number having doubled in the past 5 years, it is clear that an increasing number of people are adopting this practice as a means of managing their overall health and improving flexibility, strength, and mind management.

Yet, with a focus on the vast majority of people who are still living stressed lives and chasing false wizards, it is important to deal with the barriers that a reluctant prospect may feel they face in deciding to start a disciplined, consistent practice.

If any of the stereotypes intimidate you, the true picture of those individuals currently practicing yoga at home, in yoga studios, and in gyms is much different, and you can be assured that you will find someone just like you. Even among the 75,000 plus yoga instructors in the U.S. alone, the demographic is becoming more representative of the overall population. Instructors range from the youngest certified teacher in the country, 11-year-old Tabay Atkins, who started practicing yoga at age 6, to 93-year-old Ronnie Arnold, who still teaches in the basement of her New York home.

Case Examples
Pre-K to High School

Newark Yoga Movement
Debby Kaminsky, Founder

Perhaps the premier initiative in the country taking mindfulness to a total community is the Newark Yoga Movement. If anything challenges the stereotype of the typical yoga practitioner, this inspiring initiative does.

To illustrate the breadth of the national crisis in education, one educator in Atlanta described her class of third graders as an environment of "cheerless chaos"! This description would not be far off the mark for many schools even into the high school grades. Detention and suspensions are the standard

punishment for disruptive behavior. Students from inner-city neighborhoods, many living in one-parent households or with a relative, have anger, stress, and resentment issues to work through. From Pre-K through the teen years, social media, cyberbullying, the pressure for grades, and extracurricular activities make this the most anxious, stressed, and pressured time ever for young people.

According to the National Institute of Mental Health, 38 percent of girls and 26 percent of boys between the ages of 13 and 17 have an anxiety disorder. In addition, teacher burnout is a pressing issue, with nearly one-third of all newly recruited teachers either resigning or reporting burnout within the first three to five years (www.Yoga4classrooms.com).

Founded in 2009 by Debby Kaminsky, a former Senior Advertising Executive, the reach and impact of the Newark initiative is truly amazing. Like so many, she found yoga transformational, and with "a servant's heart", decided to take it to others. In addition to her work here, she has taught yoga in Kenya, Tanzania, and Israel.

The following illustrates their amazing reach and impact they have had

- 30,000 students, with 76 percent saying they enjoyed
  and benefitted, and
- 3,500 educators, with 90 percent saying yoga made their jobs easier.

Several free yoga classes are provided in the Newark community each week in unique venues—the Newark Museum, the public library, parks, community centers—so that those who are unable to afford to pay for classes can participate, as everyone can, in breathing and yoga.

They have helped launch other similar models in Atlanta and Indianapolis, and stand at the ready to help others if asked.

College Students

After going to college, in some ways the stresses of the teen years and of getting into a student's college of choice have abated, only to be replaced with the loneliness of being away from home for the first time, making new friends, and trying to decide on a major field of study. "Research done at Guilford College shows that college students who practice yoga exhibit reduced confusion, tension, anger and depression." Graduates are moving into a world of fast-paced change and innovation that will require much agility and mental balance in order to stay centered and able to reinvent their job and professional skills in order to stay current with rapidly evolving job markets.

A Man Who Thinks Yoga Is Not Macho Enough

Any man who has played or watched sports has heard a coach tell a player, "You need to slow the game down." Stress in a high-pressure "win or lose moment" in a game can neutralize the strength and speed advantage that one player or team may have over the other. For any man who thinks yoga is not masculine enough, the number and range of teams and individual players adopting yoga and meditation is growing rapidly. There is increasing realization that greater flexibility and *particularly a calm* mind in many cases, can provide the competitive edge. (See below on professional teams and athletes.)

She-roes: Wonder Women on the High-Wire
Casey Williams, Dawn Scott, and Mari Woodlief

The last several decades have seen a significant paradigm shift for women and their role in society at large. The operative cliché for women, even the college educated up to the late 1960s, was "Work hard for your Mrs. degree, have children, and support your husband in his primary role as the main breadwinner for the family."

High divorce rates, single parenthood, and the feminist movement have all contributed to this shift in the traditional role of women. In some cases, women are being forced to move outside of the traditional role, even if that would not be their preference. Broken relationships force some into becoming their own single source of financial support. In a growing number of cases, women are choosing to "have it all"—a career, children, and an active role in their community and society at large.

This "Wonder Woman" choice brings purpose to one's life but also high levels of anxiety, stress, and pressure. The glass ceiling still impedes career and pay rates, and most job environments are still male-dominated, with all that this brings. Sexual harassment, and a premium on a woman's looks, mode of dress, and so on, along with a feeling that "I have to outperform all the men, in order to just be considered an equal" add to the pressure cooker of the Wonder Woman career choice.

Yet, many succeed and prosper in spite of all of this. What goes unseen, however, behind the outward appearance of "having it all together", are the extraordinary measures taken by these women to keep pace with all the demands this role places on them.

Casey Williams

Raised by a single mother, Casey Williams is a 36-year-old woman from Dallas, married with three daughters. On top of her full-time job, she and husband Gregory operate a catering business. She teaches manners and etiquette classes to young girls in various mentor programs and volunteers with Helping Hands to feed the homeless, with Boys and Girls Club of Dallas to help out with activities, and with Girls That Twirl Majorettes to do fundraising.

"Yoga has become very important to me, I am very busy! I have been on a constant race for the last six years. Balancing school, my job, volunteering, church, and family life, I have very little time for myself. In spite of the tremendous stress I'm under. Drugs and alcohol are not options for me. My relationship with God and prayer helps. But I needed a physical release.

"I heard about Yoga N Da Hood! What in the world is this? I was curious! I asked if kids could come and was told yes... AND I FELL IN LOVE! It was so relaxing and calming. My spirit felt better, and my daughters were calm.

I found my answer to coping with the daily stress of job and family. I decided to get my girls into yoga because, any activity that they are a part of, I am a part of. I want to teach them a way to cope with pressure and stress, and be able to channel their energy into something positive instead of negative.

"Courtlynn was diagnosed with autism spectrum disorder last year. This has been a very stressful for us all as we learn how to deal with behaviors and meltdowns as a family unit. Yoga helps keep her calm, and concentrating on the movements and values helps her to be at peace. It is like therapy for her! Kaitlynn was diagnosed with asthma and severe allergies. She has been disabled since the age of four with constant hospital visits and admissions. Having two daughters with special needs can be very challenging, but I know that yoga is the answer for all of us!

"Kamryn is eight years old, a talented and gifted student and an avid soccer player. My girls enjoy going to yoga. It is relaxing for them. They have their share of arguments and disagreements. But this is something that they can use to channel their energy."

The girls in their own words:

Kamryn: "I think that it is fantastic because you get relaxation. I think it is awesome because I can stretch out my body so it won't be very tired."

Courtlynn: "I really, really like it and give it 1,000 likes. I want to go every day and I am ready to go again. I like being with my mom and sisters."

Kaitlynn: "I like the stretching part of yoga. I like the way my body is comfortable and relaxing. I feel happy when I go. Sometimes I itch and sneeze when I am outside, but I like going."

Dawn Scott

Dawn Scott is the award-winning lead news anchor for THV11, the CBS affiliate in Little Rock, Arkansas. She has been repeatedly voted "Best News Anchor" by readers of Arkansas's largest statewide newspaper, the *Arkansas Democrat-Gazette*. She has also won the Edward R. Murrow award and two Emmy awards.

A graduate of Northwestern University, her aspiration for as long as she can remember was to be a television reporter. "I've always been curious about the news, and felt that having this front-row seat to life, was incredibly exciting." Yet, in her own words there was and remains a "dark side" to her life that to this day requires vigilance. Alcohol has deep roots on both sides of her family tree. Her father, a football player, devastated by being cut by the Oakland Raiders in the early 1970s, turned to both alcohol and drugs to cope with his dream being destroyed. Her mother divorced him before

Dawn really knew him, and her mother became an alcoholic in her efforts to cope with being a single mother with a young child to support. Her mother is now sober and has maintained sobriety since 1983.

Following her dream to become a TV reporter, she looked for jobs and was repeatedly disappointed, but finally was hired at a station in Cedar Rapids, Iowa, only to have her father, also living in Iowa then, die of a heart attack at age 44. At age 24, Dawn became even more anxious and depressed. "When I was on the air, I was calm, but I was getting anxiety attacks day and night. I started drinking wine, but knew I was playing with fire, given my family history."

Prior to getting married and moving to Seattle, she discovered yoga. "It literally changed my life. I walked out of my first session, and it was like a miracle cure. I felt calm."

She became a certified yoga instructor and taught yoga for five years, while also continuing her broadcast career. During her 11-year marriage, she had two children, and yet had another life-changing event to face: A divorce in 2013.

While having to keep a good public face for her daily newscast, the daily realities off-camera were quite different—more anxiety attacks! Knowing the life-changing impact yoga had already had on her life, she stepped up her practice, and to this day still maintains a personal regimen of three to five classes per week. In addition, like Dorothy, who had Toto for her trek along the Yellow Brick Road, three months after Dawn's divorce, she got Scout, her beloved Golden Retriever, and still says, now four years later, "I'm not sure whether I rescued him or he rescued me."

With all the outward signs of success, Dawn remains mindful of the "alcohol gene" that may still lurk, and knows first-hand the allure of the "false wizards" and the need to self-regulate the anxiety and pressure that come with the career choice she has made and with her family history.

Mari Woodlief

She made the choice to "have it all" and, like most women who have, has dealt with all the hurdles and barriers that go with that choice. The lead headline in *D Magazine*, recently referred to her as "The Most Powerful Woman in Dallas Politics", and arguably as the most powerful behind the scenes, non-elected official in its history. She is the Chief Executive and Co-Owner of Allyn Media, and has served as chief strategist of several successful candidate and issue-related campaigns. In this same article, she was referred to as "painfully quiet, but brilliant".

In spite of her degree in foreign service and anthropology, and her drive and ambition, just out of college, she took jobs waiting tables and working as a volunteer in political campaigns before finally finding her footing at Allyn Media as a receptionist. After playing a lead role in the successful campaign of Vicente Fox for President of Mexico, the company was sold to Fleishman Hillard, with Mari ascending to the role of President. Subsequently, she and her partner bought the company, and continue to own and run it today.

What a story! From waiting tables and answering the phones to owning the company, being a single mother, and being the driving force behind so many successful, high-profile people and initiatives. She is an entrepreneur in both the traditional sense and in a larger, and even more impactful, human sense.

Like many women, the effort required to hurdle all the barriers to the top leave many reaching a moment of truth in their life where it's time to "focus on me and my well-being" for the first time in a long time.

Mari discovered meditation a few years ago and hired a coach who came to her house for individual sessions. This helped enormously in creating more balance and equilibrium for a pace that had become frenetic. Her conviction on the advantage of yoga practice was sealed when she saw the healing impact it had on a friend who was in rehab and trying to recover from a major mental health crisis.

She and her partner in Allyn Media have opened Mastermind, a "gym for the brain". "You can have everything, but mental imbalance, unaddressed, can take you down," she says. They are partnering with the Brain Performance Institute at the University of Texas at Dallas on a number of initiatives, and are preparing a number of "big-impact applications focused on police, nonprofits, colleges and universities, and corporations. Financially secure, healthy and grounded, she sees mind-health challenges in every direction and is determined to bring her personal experience in its healing powers to those around her—colleagues, friends, and strangers.

Mari and the Love of her life, her son Owen

Veterans with PTSD

The traumas for those coming home from war have gotten more and more press coverage as time has gone by. The U.S. Department of Veterans Affairs and a number of private organizations, like the Warrior Spirit Project (see profile in Chapter 9) are using yoga and meditation with impressive results.

There are several definitions of trauma. One used by the Warrior Spirit Project is "any event or series of events that leave you feeling overwhelmed, helpless, and fearful for your own life/safety or for someone close to you". These events can be a single event, repeated events, or extended ones. As discussed in Chapter 3, the brain tries to process an event but cannot because the prefrontal cortex gets flooded with cortisol and is shut down by the overstimulated amygdala. A returning veteran, having experienced a traumatic event, will have a low tolerance for any subsequent event that triggers a response, and can then go into deep depression and cause self-harm or harm to others.

Orlando Garcia

An American warrior in the best and true sense of the word, he served three deployments in the first Gulf War, including Desert Storm and Desert Shield, and then 12 years later, served two deployments in Iraq as a First Sergeant in the infantry. Like many, he came back with both physical injuries and injuries to his spirit and mind. As a consequence, he was assigned to a Warriors Transition Unit (WTU) along with others having similar injuries. This was his first introduction to yoga.

"I didn't realize at first how much damage the war had done to my spirit and psyche. It took me nine months to open up and be able to talk about it. I had lost eight of my "boys" to roadside IEDs. I had deep-seated survivor's guilt and refused the Purple Heart, because they gave their lives—I was injured, but I survived." Adding to the mental burden was the final straw: His request to return to the war zone was denied by his Sergeant Major, who said, "Not to this unit." "They saw me as damaged goods, and had no further use for me. I retired after 23.5 years."

He says that yoga and the Warrior Spirit Project have been a godsend. "I still struggle with anxiety and depression, but the guidance I get to 'just breathe' and don't worry about the poses calms me immensely." He credits his yoga family for saving him from being another military suicide.

An Already Fit Amateur or Professional Athlete

Most every team in all the major sports leagues have leading-edge gym equipment and employ multitudes of fitness trainers. But an increasing number of people are discovering that the mental game is really the competitive edge. Additionally, in the hyperactive social media world that envelops public figures of all types, being able to deal with the scrutiny and 24/7 coverage of all that you and your team do is an important dimension as well.

Ricky Williams

Ricky Williams is known widely as one of the most gifted football players of his generation, a two-time All American at the University of Texas, a Heisman Trophy winner, and an All-Pro running back in the NFL. He holds the important distinction of being the only Heisman winner to also earn a certification in yoga instruction.

Ricky has experienced the peaks of fame and all that comes with that. Unknown at the time was the darkness he was dealing with on an intensely personal level.

A social anxiety disorder and borderline personality disorder, along with the pressures of getting an education and performing at a high level in the

Ricky instructing and the author doing the demos

NFL were bringing more and more darkness into his life. Being rich and famous, with its many perks, was becoming too much to handle without medication, and later he used marijuana to help him cope. Three suspensions for failed drug tests, and the embarrassment from that, finally moved him to retire from football.

Searching, like us all, for life's most elusive condition (peace of mind), he discovered yoga and was so taken with the peace and calm that he experienced, that he went to India to study with a master. He went through a grueling yoga instructor certification regimen and earned his official certificate to teach. He taught free classes in Toronto during his one season in the Canadian Football League. His life is now dedicated to healing and educating others with disorders through the Ricky Williams Foundation and other initiatives.

Teams and Players Adopting Yoga

- The New York Giants, the Seattle Seahawks, and the Golden State Warriors are examples of teams practicing yoga. Golden State Coach, Steve Kerr, an innovative thinker on several fronts, has led the initiative to incorporate the practice into his team's overall workouts.
- LeBron James, widely considered to be the best basketball player in the NBA, is a dedicated practitioner, and he says increased strength and flexibility are the reasons, but, he adds, "It's not just about the body, it's also about the mind, and the ability to stay focused."
- Tom Brady of the five-time Super Bowl champions the New England Patriots gives his yoga practice credit for helping him with both flexibility and being able to manage the mental side of the game.
- Russell Wilson, quarterback of the Super Bowl champion the Seattle Seahawks is a devoted practitioner.
- Kyle Hendricks and Cy Young Award winner Jake Arietta of the World Series champion the Chicago Cubs are both devoted to yoga and meditation as a part of their overall mind–body fitness regimens.

To conclude this section on athletes, the prize for "out-of-the-box" thinking should go to the Washington Capitals of the National Hockey League, who have started offering free yoga sessions to their fans to help them manage the tense times leading up to the Stanley Cup Playoffs.

Like the pre-2016 Chicago Cubs, the Capitals have a history of getting close, raising fan expectations, and then flaming out at the end. The Cubs hadn't won the World Series since 1908—due to the infamous Billy Goat curse put on Wrigley Field in the 1945 World Series. A third-generation Cubs fan was quoted a few years back as saying, "They killed my grandfather, they got my father, and now they're working on me." If only Cubs management had been as far-sighted as the Washington Capitals management, there's no telling how many lives might have been saved!

A Celebrity

Celebrities are generally paid well and catered to, yet they worry about getting their next role and if there will be one, about maintaining their "looks", about being trailed by the paparazzi, about dealing with fabricated headline stories in the tabloids, and the list goes on. The stories of substance abuse and overdose are legion, and require no further elaboration here to make the point. In spite of those who try to cope with alcohol, drugs, and other substances, an increasing number people are turning to yoga and meditation:

An example is Russell Brand, who not only practices yoga but also is a certified instructor. Additionally, Reese Witherspoon, Naomi Watts, Julia Roberts, Halle Berry, Nicole Kidman, Jessica Biel, Brooke Shields, Helen Hunt, Drew Barrymore, Matthew McConaughey, Gwyneth Paltrow, Jennifer Aniston, Sting, among others.

Many of those in show business and entertainment, particularly the top performers, are learning that talent, charm, and good looks may launch a career but won't sustain one, and like high-performing athletes, they have added mindful movement and meditation to their lives as a means of self-regulation.

A Business Executive: Fiddlers on the Roof!

The acceleration in speed of the cycle of innovation will not abate and will likely increase in the near to medium term. The forces of creative destruction that have produced so much obsolescence in such a relatively short period of time will continue and will remain a source of anxiety from the daily operations floor to the C-suite. It should be noted that the length of tenure mortality rate among CEOs is also at an all-time high. Companies are dealing with constant innovation on the part of competitors, impatient boards, and shareholders.

Like Tevye in *Fiddler on the Roof,* today's CEO stands straddling the top of the barn, trying not to fall, playing and hoping the music continues to sound sweet—happy shareholders, a patient board, and flattering articles in the business press. Tevye lived in Tsarist Russia in an easier time, but was besieged on all sides by a hostile tsar, weather that could decimate his crops at any time, village boys with lustful designs on his daughters, and a wife whom he felt didn't appreciate his finer qualities. Today's CEO faces different, but just as threatening, challenges. Perhaps the biggest, is "Will I survive my success?"—a question coined by life coach Max Strom.

I Hate My Job!

The latest Gallup survey shows that a full two-thirds of people are disengaged at work. The consequences are high absenteeism rates, staff turnover, and poor customer service. This is a cancer on productivity and overall company performance, and requires leadership from the top.

Some CEOs are stepping out and organizing yoga and meditation sessions for employees, and some are actively participating in these sessions, which create a sense of camaraderie on top of other benefits. One CEO says, "As a father of four and being the CEO of a large company, can be very stressful, and the relief from doing the downward dog (yoga pose) for me and our employees provides a relaxing break from our constant drive to outperform our competitors."

Benefits to companies and employees

- Facilitates teamwork
- Keeps stress levels low and energy levels high

- Improves engagement
- Boosts morale
- Calmer minds make better decisions

A number of large companies like General Mills, Goldman Sachs, and Aetna are in the vanguard of this movement to get their employees engaged in mindful movement. Aetna's program is designed to improve overall well-being, and is being led from the top by its CEO, Mark Bertolini. He has offered free yoga and meditation classes to Aetna's employees, and more than 13,000 have participated.

A Senior Going Gently Into that Good Night

"Go not gently into that good night... rage, rage against the dying of the light." This opening line from the iconic poem by the Welsh poet Dylan Thomas should be the mantra of all seniors, yet the vast majority start yielding to psychological aging long before physical aging presents any significant barriers to participating in movement activities. It is encouraging to see from recent statistics released by the American Association of Retired People (AARP) that of those currently doing yoga, almost 40 percent are over 50.

Fred Sommese

An 88-year-old marine veteran of World War II and Korea, Fred is the very embodiment of someone who practices a disciplined regimen to self-regulate his life and health and to control how he responds to the stresses and strains that life brings. "I learned the virtues of discipline in the Marine Corps, and that lesson has never left me." He has chosen not to "go gently into that good night" but to practice each week a regimen of chair yoga

Fred in Chair Yoga class.

plus another three days per week of walking one mile on the gym treadmill and doing upper-body work in weight training. Of his yoga practice, he says, like so many, "It is different, and I feel different, calmer and more flexible." Anyone who is curious about yoga but thinks, "No one my age does yoga," only has to look at Fred and his other friends in his church yoga class to probably find someone just like them.

Several of the large insurance companies participate in the Silver Sneakers program, which fully pays for a gym membership at several of the leading national gym chains. Most of these offer yoga classes, including those especially for seniors.

Benefits of Yoga to Seniors:

- Anxiety reduction
- Reduces high blood pressure
- Improves flexibility and joint health
- Balance and stability improvement
- Improved respiration

Source: Chopra Center for Wellness

As a reminder of what was discussed in Chapter 6, "Watch your self-talk! You are not your age!", what greater inspiration is there than the 93-year-old Ronnie Arnold, who not only still teaches a weekly class but also has been a committed yoga practitioner since 1973. She says of her early days, "I've never had such a special movement in my life. It was indescribable what I felt. It was on such a level that was so deep and profound. It was life-changing." Such comments are not atypical from both young and old. In Chapter 10, there is a list of resources that seniors can access to get started, including resources for those who may be confined to a wheelchair, but who can still participate in Chair Yoga, which provides good upper-body movement and many of the same benefits of traditional yoga.

CHAPTER 9

Maybe... Later... Never! Can Be Now and Forever—Your 66-Day Commitment

I f "*Maybe* I'll do it" or "I will do it *later*" ends up being never in your life, like it does with so many of us, this is now the MOMENT OF TRUTH—your very own Lucy moment: Committing to a program of your own!

CLARITY, FOCUS, AND EXECUTION!

Be clear that you are committed to changing your life.

Focus on why and how to do this.

Execute each day with yoga and/or meditation.

Disciplined Execution of Your Program:
66-Day Commitment

———————✳———————

"In the war between the rock and the river,
the river always wins."

—*Chinese Proverb*

———————✳———————

Commit to the activity with a promise to yourself to take charge of your own stress management, no matter what!

Just as the relentless flow of the river finally wears the rock down and forces it to give way, so can your commitment to changing your life. You can tame the monkey! More of success in life comes from persistence and sweat than from brilliance! Like everything else, reaping the benefits of this true life-changing regimen involves committing to and making this practice a "without fail" part of your daily life.

The *Yoga Beginners Bible* says, "Research by the University College London shows that it takes on average 66 days of consistently doing something for it to become a habit." Each day, remind yourself about "Why am I doing this?" Hopefully, now that all the benefits are better known to you, this won't be a difficult question to answer. Commit to the activity with a promise to yourself to take charge of your own stress management, no matter what!

For those who are skeptical or reluctant, I suggest starting with a focus on breath and meditation first for a few weeks. This will be a big first step in seeing the calming benefits. For those only able to do chair yoga, this can be an excellent way to get started. Yoga Nidra is a particularly good beginning point for experiencing the restorative benefits of mindful breathing. All it requires is lying down, closing the eyes, and breathing for 20 minutes or so. It helps if you access a guided session by simply googling. Yoga Nidra, where you will find a number of options.

For other people, commit to yoga three days per week and a 20-minute meditation session each day. Start with a set of poses that you can do, and, again, *go to your limit, not past it*. Other ways to pursue this are to find an accountability partner to do it with or to split your meditation sessions into two separate ones if that is easier.

> **The monkey never takes a break, and is our lifelong companion. Keeping him in his cage and under control requires commitment to a consistent daily regimen.**

Since the focus of this book is the new convert, who can easily get confused with all the many choices of yoga available, some guidance may be in order in order to ensure a good start that will endure as part of an ongoing, life-long yoga and meditation practice.

The monkey never takes a break, and is our lifelong companion. Keeping him in his cage and under control requires commitment to a consistent daily regimen.

This may sound daunting, but is actually quite manageable, even for those with jobs that are very demanding, and even for those who traveling from city to city during the week. The flexibility, strength, and balance benefits can be achieved for most people with a 3-day per week, 45-minute to one-hour yoga session.

As time goes by and you get more accustomed to the daily flow of things, you may find, as I have, that you want to meditate twice per day for twenty minutes each time, and start each day, even your off days from the formal class, with four to five of the more basic poses in order to get the blood and brain chemicals flowing, and to provide a little "oil for the joints".

The Program

Which Type of Yoga

With any of these choices, you will increase flexibility, strength, balance, and posture, improve your sleep and energy levels, detoxify your organs, and release the natural calming brain chemicals that bring the ultimate reward, the hydrated, cleansed and blissful state—the Emerald City!

As your initial practice becomes consistent and more comfortable, you may want to explore some of the other styles, but as a starting point, Vinyasa Flow is probably the best choice for the beginner.

- **Vinyasa:** This is a synchronized style that can be either slow and deliberate, or fast and vigorous, depending on the instructor. The "one breath, one movement" feature is designed to create a continuous flow or segue from one pose to the next, and brings with it all things necessary to unite body, mind, and spirit over the course of a 45 to 60-minute session. A Vinyasa class starting with a 4 to 5-minute breathing, healing meditation and ending with a 4 to 5-minute Shavasana provides a good blend of postures, mindful breathing, detoxing, and meditation.

- **Power Yoga:** This is sometimes also referred to as "gym yoga" because of its popularity among those already reasonably fit and desiring to become more flexible and balanced. It is usually fast paced, and is a more vigorous version of Vinyasa Flow. The already-fit beginner will find it to be a good aerobic workout, and will be very pleased with the focus on poses that promote the desired flexibility and balance improvements.

- **Yin Yoga:** Also known as restorative yoga, this should be a part of the repertoire in anyone's practice because of its stress on a calm session, including soft meditation music, and holding the individual poses for three to five minutes each. The importance of this is that it provides a gentle, yet sustained and effective, stretch to the fascia. The fascia get little emphasis or discussion in fitness circles, yet they are very important to the organs, joints, and ligaments in particular. The fascia is a "thin sheath of fibrous tissue enclosing a muscle or other organ". Put more simply, it is the body's connective tissue.

Where to Start Your Practice

The doubling of the numbers of those practicing yoga over the past few years has also resulted in a major expansion in the number of locations, including single-purpose yoga studios and multi-purpose gyms and recreation centers. There has also been a big jump in home practice. If a location is available near your home, that is the best choice, because having a certified instructor to provide guidance at the start is valuable. If such a place is not available, there are many apps and online courses and instructors available for the home practice. A list is available in Chapter 10.

Beginner's Checklist

- Research for style, studio, and teacher.
- Bring a mat and towel.
- Avoid peer comparisons. All were beginners once.
- Be prepared for stumbles and minor falls.
- Remember that breathing is first and foremost.
- Go with a friend if one is available.
- Sit in the back if that makes you more comfortable.
- Sit in the front, and be surprised at the warm welcome you will receive.

What Type of Meditation

Even a few good breaths will help induce calming a stressful situation.

The calming effects of meditation can be achieved through any one of several methods, and like the app and online resources available to the home practitioner for yoga, there are numerous apps available (see Chapter 10). These range from the beginning meditator to the more experienced one. Please refer back to Chapter 7 for more detailed instructions and suggestions.

There are other versions of the seated position, including the Lotus Position. Sitting upright on a chair, with your back and shoulders straight, and your hands resting comfortably on the knees will also work. The most important thing is to close the eyes and start with mindful breathing, with the goal of getting into the "now". A good target for time is 20 minutes, although in a rush, even a few good breaths will help induce calming a stressful situation.

Breathing

In Chapter 3, the various mindful breathing techniques are outlined. The challenge, even for the experienced practitioner, is to keep the mind focused on the breath. The Darth Vader or Ocean Breath method of breathing in and out of the visualized hole in the throat is a good way to keep the focus on the "now". This is the most recommended method, although not the only one.

Equipment

The minimum requirement is a yoga mat, which many gyms and studios provide, or, if you are practicing at home, a carpeted floor will work. Mats and other equipment are easy to find on Amazon or other online sites. Yoga blocks and straps aren't a necessity but can be a good idea, as they can be a big help to the beginner as he or she learns to get into the poses and hold them. You should wear comfortable clothing, something well-fitted enough to avoid stepping on your cuffs if you wear long leggings, or having a blousy shirt drop down over your head and block your view when doing some of the poses.

CHAPTER 10

Yoga Evangelism: Yoga Is Not a Religion—It Is MIND and BODY Health!

Spreading the Good News

...And now a message and a plea to all who are already practicing and experiencing the awesome benefits of a yoga practice: Please help take the message to those most in need. There is a national crisis and we can do something big and impactful in helping to deal with it.

At the risk of contributing to the already confused and mistaken notion that yoga is a cult or a religion, I want to borrow a term, "evangelism". I feel this best describes the effort needed to spread the word among those who direly need tools and methods to regulate and manage their stressful lives, and to cope with the pressures of adapting to life in the A.S.A.P. Lane and to the "future shock" described in the opening chapters.

In its generic sense, evangelism refers to "preaching the gospel, and winning converts" through a proactive recruitment movement led by those already converted and zealous enough to be willing to share the message with others. The term "gospel" itself means good news, and the vast majority of those approximately 40 million people in North America already practicing yoga and meditation, speak of it already as "life changing".

Ebony Smith and Yoga N Da Hood

Inspired by the (see Chapter 1) life-changing effect of yoga in her own life, Ebony is the true embodiment of a yoga evangelist. She formed a nonprofit, Yoga N Da Hood, with the mission of taking yoga and mindfulness to underserved communities. She offers "no cost" yoga and compassion workshops to groups ranging from young schoolboys and girls to adults of all ages. I have participated in her "Saturday in the Park" sessions, and it is truly inspirational to see 125 yoga mats with people of all ages and body types spread out over an acre or so of parkland. Many come with the stereotype in mind of difficult, if not undoable, poses, and are surprised to learn that since they can breathe, they can do yoga. Because many are frightened away by pictures they have seen in magazines, Ebony "promises no headstands".

Unlike the world's major religions that preach salvation as the ultimate step in preparing for the next life, yoga and meditation make no promises or claims about the next life, only the promise of managing and self-regulating "now" without the crutches provided by the false wizards.

Ebony Smith and Author

To put at ease those who think it is a religion, there are multitudes, indeed millions, of Christians, Jews, Muslims, Hindus, and Buddhists who currently practice yoga and meditation and still practice their religious faith.

The yoga evangelist, having made their own journey, will already understand many, if not most, of the reasons and excuses that will be encountered in delivering a "conversion message" to someone. Later in this chapter, you will find a list of objections normally encountered, and some suggestions on how to deal with them.

The Yoga and Meditation Gospel:

- If you can breathe, you can do yoga.
- Mindful breathing is the Yellow Brick Road.
- Manage stress one breath at a time.
- The time is always just NOW.
- MAKE time for health now, or FIND time for stress and illness later.

- My own natural brain chemicals are my wizards.
- Fitness is mind, body, and spirit, not just physical.
- Commit to consistent practice; the monkey never rests.
- Do only what you can do; go to your limit, not past it.
- First and foremost, have a calm mind, then strength, flexibility, and balance.
- You are not your age.

In the first chapter, I mentioned the "modest ambition" of this book being to play some part in helping launch a mass movement to bring into the fold those among us who are suffering in silence or using the crutch of the false wizards.

There is an epidemic of crisis proportions, and a "viral spread" among those not practicing today would be a true game changer.

Nancy Loera

An emigrant from Mexico, Nancy came to the United States 15 years ago, speaking virtually no English, but full of hope for the future. On Thanksgiving 2004, her husband left, and she was soon homeless. "I felt like my life was over, I was numb, virtually without hope, and to boot spoke very little English." A woman at her church directed her to the Salvation Army. "Sobbing, I took the bus, arrived, and that's where my grace began." She received the basics of food, shelter, and love. She remembers a day at the playground, telling herself that when her

> There is an epidemic of crisis proportions, and a "viral spread" among those not practicing today would be a true game changer.

life got better and her English improved, she would pay it forward. At the time, she had no idea that yoga was in her future, but once she started her own practice, in her own words, "It grounds me, soothes me, nurtures me, and allows me to 'let go'. I have found that I can overcome anything one breath at a time."

Nancy is paying it forward by leading yoga and Zumba classes at the same Salvation Army location that took her in. She says there is a big need among the Latino population, and there is a challenge to instruct in Spanish, since most of the poses don't have a direct translation from English to Spanish. In a letter of testimony from the volunteer supervisor, she is credited with not only bringing fitness instruction to the residents but also is "a light in the life of all these individuals". This is yoga evangelism at its best.

If each of the current, nearly 40 million practitioners would add "yoga evangelism" to their practice and commit to spreading the gospel (good news) and making just 3 new converts over the next 12 months, that would create a threefold increase in the current number of those proactively managing their body-mind fitness.

Extrapolated over time, yoga and meditation would become a part of every single man, woman, and child's daily regimen. This would truly be a physical and mental health revolution.

The effect among those not yet suffering from some stress-related acute mental condition would be immediate. For trauma survivors and others with more debilitating conditions, it would take longer, but the first step would have been taken, with virtual certainty that relief was on the way. As related in other chapters, increasing scientific evidence and the personal testimony of those who have already experienced the healing effects of yoga and meditation provide enough proof to give each "evangelist" a compelling message to use with a new prospective convert.

The Warrior Spirit Project

Trauma among returning military veterans and first responders has increasingly become an issue being addressed by a number of nonprofit organizations. Working in partnership with the Brain Performance Institute

at the University of Texas at Dallas, Charla and David Trusdale provide, at no cost, trauma-sensitive yoga and meditation to veterans and first responders. From a family of marines, David served in the Naval Criminal Investigative Service, including stints in Afghanistan and Iraq. As a couple, they served a stint in Japan and at GITMO. During David's time in Afghanistan and Iraq, Charla was pursuing her career as a fitness trainer and wellness director. Like so many, she discovered that physical fitness needed mind fitness to go along with it, in order to truly be able to say, "I'm fit." She discovered yoga in 1993, and knew right away that it was "different".

Knowing firsthand that "no one comes back from these war zones unchanged", following David's retirement, they founded the nonprofit Warrior Spirit Project. Charla says, "A broken spirit can be more harmful than a broken body." As their website states, "We believe that post-traumatic stress is not a disorder to be managed, but an injury receptive to healing," They provide "yoga, dogs, and dirt", using support dogs and community gardening, along with "trauma-sensitive yoga". This type of yoga is different from any normal yoga session—no music, no touching, no walking around by the instructor, and so on. All this provided at no cost to veterans and first responders. Both Charla and David are now certified yoga instructors and also trained in the highly specialized Warriors at Ease methodology.

Ministers, rabbis, imams, lamas, and other "holy men" are often left with a much harder task—persuading the unconverted to take the 'leap of faith'. Faith is defined in the New Testament as "the substance of things hoped for, the evidence of things not seen". With yoga and meditation, there is enough "here and now" evidence to present to a new prospective convert.

Dealing with the Excuses and Reasons

The demographic makeup of non-practitioners cuts across age, gender, and class lines. It includes many who are already doing some things to improve their health, but haven't made the connection that fitness and health are mind and body connected. This group will be an easier "sell" once the dots are connected for them. They will already understand to some extent the "endorphin high" that exercise brings.

When they understand the yoga glow, radiance, hydration, or state of "bliss" created by the full shot of natural brain chemicals, activated and transmitted through each organ of the body by the vagus nerve, they will require less persuasion than those who are not currently physically active. The strength, flexibility, and balance benefits will resonate with this group right away.

Glen Delgado story

Born in Puerto Rico, and the son of a retired lieutenant colonel in the U.S. Army, Glen is a 33-year-old Dallas policeman. Buff and fit, and a long-time practitioner of aerobic and weight-training activities, he says, "Yoga is different." Introduced to it by his wife, he, like so many, has discovered the benefits over and above the endorphin high that is always a part of a vigorous run or weight-training session. He finds the calming effect of a yoga session palpable. His work life is more stressful, particularly since the multiple police killings in downtown Dallas in 2016. In addition, he is a captain in the Army Reserves, and the father of a happy and active three-year-old, who joins in the yoga sessions at home with him and his wife. Like Ebony Smith, Glen, having discovered the yoga magic himself, is taking it to others through his activities in the Police Athletic League.

There is a difference between reasons and excuses. Reasons are sincerely felt but, in many cases, are misunderstood factors, while excuses are laziness disguised as reasons. The "sales pitch" or message will need to be tailored to the audience. The evangelist needs to be prepared to address some or all of the following objections:

- **I'm not flexible.** This attitude will be encountered with both the currently active and the non-active. Physical and mental flexibility are benefits of yoga and meditation, and most people aspire to this, but they may feel intimidated by the pictures and stereotypes they have in their mind. Yoga instructors, as a part of their initial 200-hour certification process, are taught to "teach those in front of you", meaning to take whatever level of experience or skill, starting with raw beginners, they find in their students and start their journey from that point.

- **I'm too busy.** An adage I heard many years ago completely spiked this one, and should resonate and give pause to anyone:

---———※———---

"Make time for exercise now, or find time for sickness later!"

---———※———---

The "stress price" we pay in damage to our health, and the days, weeks, months, and years lost to worry, rumination, anxiety, and the like are enough to motivate most people if they are persuaded of the benefits of a yoga and meditation practice. As already outlined, the time commitment for a very effective regimen would be something like 20 minutes each day for meditation and a commitment to yoga three times per week.

- **It's too hard.** Like so many of the excuses and reasons given, this one is a product of the stereotype mentioned earlier. In fact, it can be as easy or as difficult as one makes it. For the raw beginner, a yoga practice can be done at home using one of the many apps available, which give detailed instruction and can be followed at one's own pace. Additionally, as mentioned before, yoga instructors are trained to be very mindful of the class or the student they are teaching at any given time, and to move through the poses at a pace comfortable for the student.

- **My body type isn't right for yoga.** This objection is normally that of someone who feels they are "too fat". There are studios around the country just for the overweight person, including some that are marketed as simply, Fat Yoga. There are many others that have done and are doing a lot to negate the body shaming that pervades so much of society. In the classes I have participated in over the years, the makeup is very diverse, and almost always includes those who don't meet any of the stereotypes of age, weight, or skill level. The fact is that no one is paying any attention to the others in class, because they are focusing on breathing and moving.

- **My church is opposed to yoga.** This objection is encountered less and less, but is one that will need to be addressed from time to time. As discussed earlier, yoga is about a regimen focused on calming the mind, creating more strength, flexibility, and balance. Furthermore, all faiths spend a lot of their "message time" on the negative effects of the false wizards, and condemning the behaviors that many of these "crutches" inspire. In fact, churches should see yoga practice as an ally in the battle against self-destructive behavior.

- **I prefer real exercise.** First, if you think it's not real exercise, and you're already pretty fit, go to a fast-moving Power Yoga session and be prepared to "eat crow" for having uttered the words "it's not a real workout"! Second, it can be an addition to an exercise regimen, if that regimen is a more traditional one focused on aerobic fitness and strength training. Running and weight training are very beneficial, and until I discovered yoga, they were my sworn-by methods of fitness training for over 40-plus years. As time goes by, you become less and less flexible, your balance declines, and joint and ligament issues become bigger problems. In addition, as mentioned before, gyms are full of physically fit people whose "monkey brains" are as hyper as anyone's and who still haven't come to appreciate that "fitness" is both body and mind fitness.

- **I will be embarrassed/I can't do the poses.** As mentioned several times, the poses are secondary to breathing. Additionally, yoga instructors and those in the class are very welcoming to newcomers, all of them having once been newcomers themselves. Those in the class are there to mindfully breathe and move. A fallback position is to practice some of the poses at home before going to your first session.

- **I'm too old.** Classes are increasingly attracting seniors, as more and more come to the realization that aging isn't an inevitable process over which there is no control. The AARP says that approximately 40 percent of current yoga participants are over 50. As mentioned above, the great *eureka* moment for me was the section in *Ageless Body, Timeless Mind* where both the biology and psychology of aging were discussed. The *eureka* was the statement that we actually have three ages: Chronological, biological, and psychological, and that the least important is our chronological as measured by our birthdate. When asked your age, the question is, which age are you asking about? Finally, as mentioned earlier, several large insurance companies offer free gym memberships through the Silver Sneakers program.

- **I'm too far gone with PTSD or a chemical dependency.** As discussed in Chapter 7, yoga and meditation are already being used widely and successfully to treat all forms of trauma. While there is lots of success to point to, recovery is a drawn-out process, and classes with a special focus on trauma survivors would be best in these cases.

- **I don't live or work near a studio or teacher.** While there are approximately 75,000 certified yoga teachers in the United States, this can be a real issue for some. Fortunately, there are a myriad of resources available for the remote or the traveling person who wants to start a practice. There are a number of excellent apps and videos available, some free and some costing a minimal amount. A list of resources is provided in Chapter 10.

- **I'm in a wheelchair and can't stand to do the poses.** This is obviously a legitimate reason and an insurmountable barrier to participating in a traditional studio or gym session. However, there are programs and instructors specifically trained to provide this specialized type of instruction. These poses can all be done from a chair or wheelchair in a seated position. Resources are identified in Chapter 10.

Appendix

Resources: The A. B. C.'s of Optimum Health

To help you on your way to a new life and better health of both the body and the mind, please take note of the tools and resources available to you. In these, along with your own disciplined dedication, you will find calmness, strength, weight loss, better sleep, better posture, more self-confidence, flexibility, balance, courage, and love. In short, all the things and more that Dorothy, the Scarecrow, the Tin Man, and the Cowardly Lion were seeking on their way to see the Wizard, now reside within, and you need only to start moving and breathing to discover them.

Apps

There are 200-plus apps in the App Store covering all styles of yoga from beginner to advanced, and including each of the recommended ones for beginners that are discussed in Chapter 8: A Program of Your Own. An app is good for either a home practice or as a reference source when practicing at home between studio sessions.

Meditation

There are 400-plus apps on meditation in the App Store, although some are both meditation and yoga focused. Meditating with appropriate music is useful for some, as it may help with the wandering-mind syndrome some people experience. Meditating in a quiet, comfortably warm place, without music, including in the outdoors, is a good choice, using the Darth Vader or the Ocean Breath method to help manage the wandering mind, as described in Chapter 3.

Websites

- Yoga MOOC: www.yogamooc.com/resources (highly-recommended)
- Yoga Alliance: www.yogaalliance.org
- Yoga Journal: www.yogajournal.com
- YogaUOnline: www.yogauonline.com
- The Chopra Center: www.chopra.com
- Gaia.com: www.gaia.com

Home Practice

For the beginner, one or more apps are important, along with a mat. Blocks and straps may also be good to have in the early stages of your practice. There are several apps especially designed for the home practice that can be found in the App Store.

Here are some of the best:

- Yoga Studio
- YogaGlo
- Pocket Yoga
- Yoga.com Studio (All-in-Yoga)
- I Am Love by Kids Yogaverse (designed for four to eight year olds)
- DailyYoga (best for those with time pressures)
- Pocket Yoga—Practice Builder (best for DIY yogis)
- DailyBurn Yoga (good for athletes)
- FitStar Yoga
- DownDog

Studios and Private Instructors

www.yjdirectory.com: This directory is available to all, and is a good resource for studios, instructors, contact information, yoga events, teacher training, and others things, including apparel and equipment. A Google search in your city, area, or zip code will also show what is available

Books

There are many, and I have found these to be good and helpful:

- *The Yoga Bible*
- *The Yoga Beginner's Bible*
- *Ageless Body, Timeless Mind*
- *Teaching Yoga*
- *The Stress-Proof Brain*
- *You Are The Universe*
- *Yoga As Medicine*
- *Yoga Anatomy,* 2nd edition
- *Fitness Yoga*
- *The Energy Medicine Yoga Prescription*

YouTube

There are many video demonstrations of poses, breathing techniques, meditation styles, and most everything else associated with yoga that can be found on YouTube. Some of us learn better by seeing a demonstration rather than hearing or reading, so YouTube can be a very valuable help to the beginner.

Acknowledgments

I have sat down on several occasions during my life to begin the long journey that writing a book becomes. These all became false starts, as the discipline required, which is approximately three hours a day in an isolated, quiet place, faded with time. It didn't help when I would walk into a bookstore and see shelves stacked to the top with books on every conceivable topic, and wonder to myself, "Does the world really need another book, when there is no way, they will ever sell all of these?" The experience gives you a newfound respect for all the writers who labor away to produce books and articles that entertain us, educate us, and inform us.

I completed the initial manuscript in 30 days, as I found myself researching and writing about something that is a critical and pressing issue, and one that I have a passion to write about and can hopefully help do something about. As I mention in the book, I started my own practice of yoga, as a means of becoming more flexible and balanced. As with many people, my years of weight training and running, and so on had taken a toll on my joints, ligaments, and fascia. I am today much more flexible and balanced. My big *eureka*—and it is the primary message of this book—has been the mind-body connection and the flood of natural "feel good" chemicals activated in the brain and circulated throughout every organ in the body by a yoga session.

ACKNOWLEDGMENTS

This is the true magic of yoga. We are not "fit" until our minds are calm and we are able to process life and its increasingly hyperactive pace without relying on the false wizards that are taking a major, and increasingly fatal, toll on our health. I have answered my own question. The world does need another book, especially this one. I hope you find it helpful in your own life.

I owe a special debt to Gerry Robert, founder and President of Black Card Books Publishing, and his amazing team who helped every step of the way. In particular, I was fortunate to have as my writing coach, Barry Spilchuk, co-author of the international bestseller *A Cup of Chicken Soup for the Soul*. His contributions are evident throughout the book. In addition, I have been influenced for over 25 years by the writings of Dr. Deepak Chopra and his work at the Chopra Center. I read the *Yoga Journal* without fail, and have been greatly influenced by it over the years.

In the course of writing this book, I have leaned heavily on the writings and resources of many:

- *Yoga Journal*
- YogauOnline
- Yoga Alliance
- Yoga For Stress and Anxiety/*Yoga Journal* online course
- The Brain Performance Institute at the University of Texas at Dallas
- www.doyogawithme.com: Types and Styles of Yoga
- *The Energy Medicine Yoga Prescription*
- The Science and Practice of Yoga
- www.mentalfloss.com: "9 Nervy Facts About Vagus Nerve"
- www.bigpictureeducation.com: "Chemicals of the Brain"
- National Survey of Drug Use and Health: "Depression in Kids Study"
- *New York Times*

- www.NPR.com
- Georgetown Law Center on Inequality and Poverty: "Gender and Trauma Study"
- Dr. Deepak Chopra
- The Chopra Center
- *Harvard Business Review*: "How Meditation Benefits CEOs"
- www.doyoudoyoga.com: "10 Famous Men Who Do Yoga"
- www.sportster.com: "Top 15 Athletes Who Do Yoga"
- VetsYoga, www.yogawarriors.com: "PTSD and Other Veterans Stress Issues"
- www.Yoga4Classrooms.com: "Teacher Burnout"
- www.osteopathic.org: "Health Benefits of Yoga"
- www.psychologytoday.com: "Vagus Nerve"
- www.mindful.org: "Meditating with Anxiety"
- www.aarp.org: "Seniors", plus assorted other articles
- *The Stress Proof Brain* by Dr. Melanie Greenberg
- *Scientific American*
- www.familydoctor.org: "The Mind/Body Connection"
- www.oprah.com: "Dr. Oz on Yoga"
- www.SI.com: "The Rise of Yoga in the NBA"
- www.scientificamerican.com: "Opioid Crisis"
- The Warrior Spirit Project
- *The Energy Medicine Yoga Prescription*

OTHER BOOKS RECOMMENDED BY BLACK CARD BOOKS

The Millionaire Mindset
How Ordinary People Can Create Extraordinary Income
Gerry Robert
ISBN: 978-1-927411-00-1

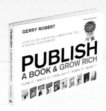

Publish a Book & Grow Rich
How to Use a Book as a Marketing Tool & Income Accelerator
Gerry Robert
ISBN: 978-1-77204-546-8

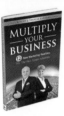

Multiply Your Business
10 New Marketing Realities for the Real Estate Industries
Gerry Robert &
Theresa Barnabei, DREC
ISBN: 978-1-77204-774-5

Image Power
Balancing Passion and Profit in Business
David McCammon
ISBN: 978-1-77204-825-4

Target Practice
8 Mistakes That Ruin a Love of the Game
Chris Dyson
ISBN: 978-1-77204-459-1

The Money Factory
How Any Woman Can Make An Extra $30,000 To $100,000 Passive Income
Lillie Cawthorn
ISBN: 978-1-77204-420-1

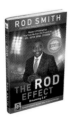

The Rod Effect
Master 8 Philosophies That Took Me from the Projects to NFL SUPER BOWL STARDOM
Rod Smith
ISBN: 978-1-77204-254-2

Sales Manager Reset
Get the Most Out of Your Sales Team
Allan Lorraine
ISBN: 978-1-77204-542-0

POWERED BY

www.blackcardbooks.com